The Political Economy of the Environment

TO BETSY, JAMIE, AND TOM

The Political Economy of the Environment

James K. Boyce

University of Massachusetts at Amherst

Edward Elgar
Cheltenham, UK • Northampton, MA, USA

Published by
Edward Elgar Publishing Limited
Glensanda House
Montpellier Parade
Cheltenham
Glos GL50 1UA
UK

Edward Elgar Publishing, Inc.
136 West Street
Suite 202
Northampton
Massachusetts 01060
USA

A catalogue record for this book
is available from the British Library

Library of Congress Cataloguing in Publication Data
Boyce, James K.
    The political economy of the environment / James K. Boyce.
        p. cm.
    Includes index.
        1. Environmental economics. I. Title.

  HD75.6 .B69 2002
  333.7—dc21

2001040216

ISBN 1 84064 366 8 (cased)

Typeset by Manton Typesetters, Louth, Lincolnshire, UK.
Printed and bound in Great Britain by MPG Books Ltd, Bodmin

Contents

Figures

Tables

Acknowledgements

Many people have assisted me during the writing of this book. I am particularly grateful to the colleagues with whom I co-authored several of its chapters: Olman Segura Bonilla (Chapter 3), Mariano Torras (Chapter 5), and Andrew Klemer, Paul Templet, and Cleve Willis (Chapter 6). Keith Griffin of the University of California, Riverside, encouraged me to bring together a number of my environmental writings into a single volume, and Edward Elgar and Alan Sturmer gave me the impetus to do so. Rachel Bouvier assisted me greatly in the nitty gritty tasks of preparing the manuscript for publication.

Earlier versions of many of these chapters appeared elsewhere. Chapter 2 was published in the journal *Disasters* (2000) under the title 'Let them eat risk: Wealth, rights, and disaster vulnerability.' Chapter 3 appeared in the volume *Investing in Natural Capital: The Ecological Economics Approach to Sustainability*, edited by Ann Mari Jansson, Monica Hammer, Carl Folke, and Robert Costanza (Washington, DC: Island Press, 1994). Chapter 4 appeared in the journal *Ecological Economics* (1994). Chapter 5 was published in *Ecological Economics* (1998) under the title 'Income, inequality, and pollution: A reassessment of the environmental Kuznets curve.' Chapter 6 also appeared in *Ecological Economics* (1999) under the title 'Power distribution, the environment, and public health: A state-level analysis.' Chapter 7 originally appeared as 'Market liberalisation, market failure,' in the Italian journal *Politica Internazionale* (1998). Chapter 8 is drawn from my book *The Philippines: The Political Economy of Growth and Impoverishment in the Marcos Era* (London: Macmillan; Honolulu: University of Hawaii Press; and Manila: Ateneo de Manila University Press, 1993). I am grateful to these publishers for permission to draw on this material.

Finally, I want to express my sincere thanks to the many individuals around the world whose struggles for a more democratic and environmentally sustainable future are a constant source of hope and inspiration.

1.   Stealing the commons

The law doth punish man or woman
that steals the goose from off the common,
but lets the greater felon loose
who steals the common from the goose.
                                        – Anonymous

Nature underpins human livelihoods both as a source of raw materials and as a sink for the disposal of our wastes. The quality of the natural environment can be profoundly affected, however, by how we distribute power and wealth among ourselves. The Earth is the home and common heritage of all humankind, but some people claim more of its bounty than others. Access to 'natural capital' – a phrase lately in vogue among economists – is filtered through our political and economic institutions. Those people who are relatively wealthy and powerful generally reap more of the benefits from uses of the environment, and bear fewer of the costs from its abuse, than do those who are relatively poor and powerless.

Disparities of power and wealth influence not only how nature's pie is sliced, but also its overall magnitude. When disparities are great, those at top of the political and economic ladder can more easily pollute the air and water and deplete the natural resource base of those at the bottom. When disparities are small, those on the bottom rungs of the shorter ladder are better able to defend themselves. A democratic distribution of power and an equitable distribution of wealth, therefore, can help to protect the environment. Conversely, an oligarchic distribution of power and an inequitable distribution of wealth can exacerbate environmental degradation.

RETHINKING THE ENVIRONMENT AND THE ECONOMY

Long before the rise of market economies, humans relied on natural resources for their livelihoods. Even today, when markets mediate access to many of the goods and services we produce and consume, much that is vital to our quality of life remains outside the sphere of market exchange. The air we breathe is not purchased at the supermarket; neither, in most cases, is the water we drink. The vast majority of the sights, smells, and sounds of daily life are not bought and sold. At the end of the day, the joys and sorrows of families and friendships often count for more than what was in our shopping baskets.

The economy is larger than the goods and services exchanged in market transactions. A broad vision of the economy takes into account all of the assets, or forms of wealth, that provide the foundation for our livelihoods; it encompasses the many dimensions of well-being that matter to us; and it embraces the full range of activities by which we derive well-being from the assets at our disposal. The economic nexus includes natural assets as well as human-made assets, non-market activities as well as market exchanges, and non-income benefits as well as income (see Figure 1.1).

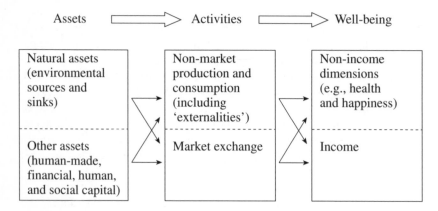

Figure 1.1   Wealth and well-being

Humans versus Nature?

Environmental debates, especially in the United States, often pit proponents of wilderness preservation against advocates of 'rational self-interest.' The preservationists typically base their case on the linkages depicted in the top half of Figure 1.1: they emphasize the crucial importance of natural assets, non-market activities, and non-income dimensions of well-being. The deep-ecology variant of the preservationist school of thought goes further, arguing that the 'rights of nature' ought to supersede human well-being as the ethical basis for policy (Nash 1990).

Those who champion rational self-interest typically base their case on the linkages depicted in the lower half of Figure 1.1. They are generally inclined to see the market as the measure of all things. Some of them recognize the need for government interventions to redress market imperfections and market failures; others claim that Adam Smith's 'invisible hand' alone delivers the greatest good to the greatest number. The libertarian variant of this school goes further, arguing not only that free markets serve to maximize human well-being, but that freedom from non-market restrictions on individual liberty should itself be an overriding social goal.

Notwithstanding their profound differences and often acrimonious disputes, both sides in this environmental debate share certain premises. Both juxtapose nature to humans, the environment to the economy, differing only in which side they think will and should ultimately prevail. The preservationists argue that, in the absence of strict controls, the magnitude of negative human impacts on the environment will overwhelm nature's capacity for resource renewal and waste assimilation. The proponents of market rationality argue that human ingenuity, guided by price signals, will triumph over environmental constraints. In addition, neither side generally devotes much concern to the well-being of the poor. In the preservationist paradigm, the poor are best fenced out of nature lest they trample upon it. In the greed-as-virtue paradigm, the poor are simply left to their free-market fates.

The starting point for this book is an alternative vision in which humans are not apart from nature, but a part of it. For thousands of years, going back at least to the origins of agriculture, human activity has shaped and reshaped the environment. As William Cronon (1995: 25) remarks, 'Nature is not nearly so natural as it seems.' The environmental impacts of human activities are often negative, but they can be positive too: we can degrade environmental quality, but we can also improve it by investing in natural capital.

In many cases, investing in natural capital takes the form of ecological restoration – repairing damages caused by earlier human activities. Examples include reforestation, the protection of endangered species to enable populations to reach levels at which they are no longer endangered, the clean-up of contaminated land and water bodies, and reductions in concentrations of air pollutants such as lead, sulfur dioxide, and suspended particulates. These investments – in effect, making amends for past 'disinvestments' in natural capital – are some of the most important ways in which humans can act to improve environmental quality.

Yet the scope for positive human impacts of environmental quality is not limited to the reversal of past damages. Humans also can, and sometimes do, enhance environmental quality above and beyond what would exist in their absence. Perhaps the greatest historic example is the domestication of crops and animals. Beginning some 10,000 years ago, human interactions with nature created rice in Asia, wheat and barley in the Near East, maize in Meso-America, potatoes in the Andes (Kahn 1985). Our daily bread, and the diverse other foods on which our survival depends, are the fruits of positive environmental changes brought about by human hands.

A more recent example is the modification of the ecosystem in the Upper Rio Grande watershed in southern Colorado and northern New Mexico. Beginning in the sixteenth century, Hispanic settlers in this bioregion constructed gravity-flow irrigation systems, known as *acequias*, that transformed arid lands into rich and diverse agricultural ecosystems. Today the descendants of these farmers maintain these water channels, thereby providing a range of valuable environmental services: soil conservation, water retention and filtration, the preservation of habitats and corridors for wildlife, and the conservation of crop genetic diversity (Peña 2001). Far from being short-sighted despoilers of nature's bounty, humans are here the 'keystone species' on whose presence the complex web of other species crucially depends.

To term the advent of crops or the creation of anthropogenic wetlands an 'improvement' in environmental quality is to make a value judgment. I believe that the basis for such judgments must be a deep commitment to the well-being of present and future generations of humankind. I embrace the goal of protecting the environment, then, not because I consider nature to be more important than people, but because I recognize that the fates of humans and nature are inextricably woven together.

Winners versus Losers

The human-versus-nature dichotomy not only neglects the potential for people to have a positive impact on the environment. It also diverts our attention from the contests *among* people that are central to an understanding of the dynamics of pollution and natural resource depletion. Environmentally degrading economic activities typically create winners, who reap net benefits from these activities, as well as losers, who bear net costs. Without the winners, these activities would not occur; without the losers, there would be little reason to worry about them, at least from the standpoint of human well-being.

To understand the reasons for environmental degradation – why more of it happens in some times and places than in others – we must ask why the winners are able to impose costs on the losers. There are three possible answers to this question:

- First, the losers may not yet exist: they belong to future generations and are not here to defend themselves. In such cases, the only feasible solution is to foster an intergenerational ethic, combining a sense of gratitude toward those who preceded us with a sense of responsibility toward those who will follow.
- Second, the losers may exist but not know it: they lack full information, for example, about the extent of air pollution and its health

impacts, and hence do not mobilize to combat it. Such cases highlight the importance of environmental research and education and of right-to-know laws that guarantee citizens access to information about environmental hazards.

- Finally, the losers may exist and be well aware that they are losers, but they lack enough power to prevent the winners from imposing environmental costs on them. In such cases, the extent of pollution and resource depletion reflects the disparity in power between the winners and the losers: the wider this disparity, the greater the amount of environmental degradation.

Empirical evidence suggests that this third explanation – in which environmental degradation is based on power disparities – is often an important part of the story. In the United States, for example, a growing number of studies indicate that low-income people and racial and ethnic minorities often face disproportionate environmental hazards (see, for example, Bullard 1994 and Pastor 2001). Internationally, countries with a more equal income distribution, greater political rights and civil liberties, and higher rates of adult literacy – indicators of a more equitable distribution of power – tend to have less air pollution, less water pollution, and wider access to clean drinking water and sanitation facilities (see Chapter 5). Within the United States, states with a more equal distribution of power (as measured by an index derived from data on voter participation, tax fairness, Medicaid access, and educational attainment) tend to have stronger environmental policies, less environmental stress, and better public health outcomes (see Chapter 6).

Poverty and the Environment

Discussions of the links between poverty and the environment often focus on the 'vicious circle' in which the poor degrade their environment in a desperate quest to survive, in turn deepening their poverty in the future. Such cases undoubtedly exist. But if much environmental degradation benefits the powerful at others' expense, then a more important link may rest on the relationship between wealth and power: poverty is bad for the environment because the poor are less able to resist having environmental costs imposed on them by the rich. In both scenarios, poverty sets the stage for environmental tragedies, but in the first case the principal actors are the poor themselves, while in the second the principal actors are the rich.

Both poverty–environment linkages can be found throughout the world. Tropical deforestation, for example, is sometimes driven by poor settlers who are clearing land on which to grow food. Other times it is driven by multinational corporations and national elites who are engaged in timber exports, mining, and cattle ranching, often to the detriment of poor people and ethnic minorities who live in or near the forest.

Some insight into which scenario is most common can be gleaned by considering the distribution of income worldwide. The United Nations Development Programme (1992: 36) has estimated that the countries whose average incomes rank in the richest 20 percent of the world's population receive 82.7 percent of global income, while the countries whose average incomes rank in the poorest 20 percent receive only 1.4 percent of world income. Average incomes in the top tier of countries are thus about 60 times greater than in the bottom tier. World income disparities are even sharper, of course, if we consider inequalities within countries. The same UN study estimates that in 1988 the richest 20 percent of individuals around the world (regardless of whether they happen to live in a high-income or low-income country) had average annual incomes of $22,800 per person, while the poorest 20 percent had annual incomes of $163 – a 140 to 1 ratio.

The amount of environmental degradation associated with a dollar's worth of production and consumption is likely to vary across individuals and countries. Whether degradation per dollar is higher for poor people or for rich people is a question on which little systematic evidence has been collected. If the amount of degradation per dollar were roughly the same for both groups, the richest 20 percent of the world's people would account for *140 times as much* environmental degradation as the poorest 20 percent. Put differently, the total amount of degradation for which the poorest fifth is responsible could equal that for which the richest fifth is responsible only if the degradation per dollar for the poor were 140 times greater – a rather implausible suggestion. This simple comparison suggests that environmental degradation driven by the economic activities of the rich is likely to surpass, by a substantial margin, that driven by the economic activities of the poor.

This is not to say that the rich have no interest in environmental protection. Clearly they do, particularly in protecting the parts of the environment where they live and play. But the demand of the rich for environmental quality is tempered by two considerations. First, since they receive a large share of the benefits from economic activities that degrade the environment, they would bear much of the cost of protecting it: they face a tradeoff between their desire for environmental protection and their desire for higher profits and cheaper consumer goods. Second, since environmental quality is not a pure public good, available in equal measure to all, the rich can seek to displace environmental costs onto lower-income communities at home and abroad.

Reductions in poverty and a narrowing of inequalities of wealth and power, therefore, can help to protect the environment, not only by diminishing the need for the poor to degrade the environment in order to survive, but also by curtailing the ability of the rich to do so at their expense.

POLITICAL ECONOMY

Economics, according to the usual textbook definition, is about the allocation of scarce resources among competing ends. Political economy includes not only economics thus defined, but something more: it is about the allocation of scarce resources not only among competing ends, but also among competing people. The distribution of wealth and income are treated as a peripheral issue in much of economics, but in political economy who has what is absolutely central. Distribution is relevant both normatively, in judging the desirability of economic outcomes, and positively, in understanding how economies work.

The conventional explanations for environmental degradation proffered by economists usually downplay the importance of political economy. The standard textbooks characterize pollution and natural resource depletion as impersonal 'negative externalities,' social costs that slip through the fingers of the market's invisible hand. Those on the receiving end of these costs just happen to be in the wrong place at the wrong time. To correct for these market failures, the textbooks prescribe a similarly impersonal remedy: government interventions in the form of regulation, taxes, or the creation of tradable emission permits. Yet governments often fail to respond efficiently to environmental externalities; indeed, sometimes they fail to respond at all. To understand why societies act to protect environmental quality in some times and places more than others, we must examine how social decisions are governed by the distribution of wealth and power.

The Tragedies of Open Access

The 'tragedy of the commons,' described in a famous article by Garrett Hardin (1968), epitomizes the distribution-blind analysis of environmental degradation. In Hardin's parable, people have free, unlimited access to common lands where they can graze their animals. Each individual reaps the full benefit of grazing his or her livestock on the open-access lands, while bearing only a small fraction of the attendant cost of thereby reducing the amount of forage remaining for all. Overgrazing is the tragic result. Hardin proposed state regulation to safeguard the commons. Market proponents have used the same analysis to argue for the privatization of common lands.

In recent years a large body of research has demonstrated the crucial difference between common property and open access. In many places throughout the world, communities have developed informal but effective rules to ensure that common-property natural resources, including grazing lands, forests, and fisheries, are used sustainably (see, for example, Ostrom 1990). Hardin's parable hence is better termed the 'tragedy of open access,' referring to free-for-all situations where rules for the joint use of common property do not exist.

In the scramble for open-access natural resources, some people are more equal than others. In open-water fisheries, for example, the advantage goes to those who can field the most ruthless extractive technologies. Similarly, everyone may have the same right to pollute the air and water, but not everyone has equal means to do so. The law that mandates the same penalty for anyone who steals a loaf of bread, whether the thief is a starving person or a millionaire, provides a hollow form of equality. So too does the fact that a poor family living downwind from a chemical factory has as much right to foul the air as the factory's owners. Open access therefore often leads to not one tragedy, but two: the abuse of environmental resources, and the 'stealing of the commons' by powerful and wealthy interests at the expense of others.

Five Dimensions of Power

Several dimensions of power are important in analyzing the ability of different economic actors to appropriate natural resources, to discharge wastes into environmental sinks, and to prevent others from doing so:

- *Purchasing power* is the dimension of power that underpins the notion of 'consumer sovereignty' in economics textbooks: in a pure market economy, the ability and willingness of individuals to pay for various goods and services determines what gets produced. Similarly, purchasing power is the foundation for the valuation of environmental goods and services – such as biodiversity conservation or cleaner air – in the 'shadow markets' of benefit-cost analysis that are meant to underpin public-sector decision-making in a world of 'optimal planning' free of distorting political influences.
- *Decision power* – the ability to prevail in contests where different people prefer different outcomes – is the most evident 'non-economic' dimension of power. For example, a government's decisions as to what pollutants to regulate, and how strictly to regulate them, is typically based not only on dispassionate calculations of the social costs and benefits of pollution control, but also on the relative strength of the lobbying efforts by proponents and opponents of regulation.
- *Agenda power* is the ability to determine which issues enter into the arena of public decision-making at all. This is a more subtle dimension of power, in that it can shape outcomes before decision power comes into play. For example, in his classic study *The Un-politics of Air Pollution*, Matthew Crenson (1971) recounts how corporate power in

the steel town of Gary, Indiana, kept the issue of air pollution off the municipal government's political agenda for many years.

- *Value power* is the ability to influence what others want, what they themselves will choose if given the opportunity to decide. This is an even subtler dimension of power, for it raises the possibility that people's wants can be shaped by the society in which they live, so as to work against their own interests (Lukes 1974). As John Kenneth Galbraith (1973: 9) once observed, in a presidential address to the American Economic Association, such power can be wielded in an effort to persuade people that pollution is 'palatable or worth the cost.'
- *Event power* is the ability to alter the circumstances in which people make choices, rather than directly determining the choices themselves. 'Externalities' are an example. Randall Bartlett (1989: 43) offers this hypothetical illustration: 'Suppose I dig a deep pit, fill it with poisonous snakes, and throw you in. I then stand on the edge of the pit and offer to sell you a ladder. To buy or not to buy is not the only question. What prior events made you need to buy, and my influence over them, are also relevant.'

Inequalities in all five dimensions of power play a role in the political economy of environmental degradation and environmental protection.

OVERVIEW OF THE FOLLOWING CHAPTERS

The essays presented in this book explore these themes, addressing both theoretical issues and empirical evidence, and drawing on experiences in various parts of the world.

Chapter 2, 'Let them eat risk,' contrasts two approaches to policies for reducing vulnerability to natural and man-made disasters. The wealth-based approach is founded on purchasing power: decisions as to how much protection to provide and to whom are based on the conventional willingness-to-pay criterion. An alternative, rights-based approach is founded on the proposition that every individual has an equal right to a clean and safe environment. Tensions between the two approaches exist in public policy around the world. History, I suggest, is on the side of the rights-based approach.

Chapter 3, 'Investing in natural and human capital,' explores the potential for expanding the stock of natural capital, particularly in the developing countries of Latin America, Asia, and Africa. Such investments are not an alternative to investing in 'human capital' through improvements in the nutritional well-being, health, and education of the poor. Rather, investments in human capital can provide a foundation for investments in natural capital.

Chapter 4, 'Inequality as a cause of environmental degradation,' develops the theoretical basis for the proposition that inequalities of power and wealth shape the overall magnitude of environmental degradation, as well as the distribution of its social costs. This implies that a more equal distribution of wealth and a more democratic distribution of power can advance the goal of environmental protection.

Chapter 5, 'Rethinking the environmental Kuznets curve,' tests this proposition by examining the determinants of international variations in air pollution, water pollution, and access to clean water and sanitation facilities. In recent years, some economists have suggested that pollution and other forms of environmental degradation display an inverted U-shaped relation to per capita income: as economic development proceeds and average incomes rise, pollution at first increases but ultimately reaches a turning point after which environmental quality improves. An examination of international variations in income distribution, literacy, and political rights and civil liberties suggests that these may be more important than average income *per se* in determining environmental outcomes.

Chapter 6, 'Power distribution, the environment, and public health,' examines interstate variations within the United States, and reaches a similar conclusion: those states with a more equal distribution of power tend to have stronger environmental policies and tend to perform better in terms of both environmental quality and public health.

Chapter 7, 'The globalization of market failure?', considers the environmental impacts of international trade, and challenges the common assumption that the main environmental threat posed by global economic integration is that dirty and unsustainable production practices in the developing countries of the 'South' will undermine relatively clean and sustainable production in the industrialized countries of the 'North'. On the contrary, the opposite can and often does occur: dirty production in the North displaces clean production in the South. Two case studies illustrate: the intensified competition between maize producers in Mexico and the United States in the wake of the 1994 North American Free Trade Agreement (NAFTA), and the competition between jute, a natural fibre produced mainly by peasants in Bangladesh, and polypropylene, a synthetic substitute produced by the international petrochemical industry.

Chapter 8, 'A squandered inheritance,' examines the dynamics of deforestation by means of a case study of the Philippines in the era of dictator Ferdinand Marcos. Like other Southeast Asian countries, the Philippines experienced rapid deforestation in the 1960s and 1970s, driven primarily by exports of tropical hardwoods to the world market. Those who benefited most from the logging industry were well-connected politicians and military officers; and those who suffered most from its consequences were poor people who lived in or near the forests. In the Philippines, as in other countries in the region, the imbalance of power between these winners and losers propelled environmental destruction on a massive scale.

Finally, Chapter 9, 'Democratizing environmental ownership,' draws some policy implications from this analysis of the political economy of the environment. Democratization – that is, movement toward a more equal distribution of power – can provide a powerful impetus to environmental protection. At the same time, environmental protection – insofar as it embodies the principle that every person has the right to a clean and healthful environment – can provide a powerful impetus to democratization.

REFERENCES

Bartlett, Randall (1989), *Economics and Power: An Inquiry into Human Relations and Markets*, Cambridge: Cambridge University Press.

Bullard, Robert D. (ed) (1994), *Environmental Justice and Communities of Color*, San Francisco: Sierra Club Books.

Crenson, Matthew (1971), *The Un-politics of Air Pollution: A Study of Non-decisionmaking in the Cities*, Baltimore, MD: Johns Hopkins University Press.

Cronon, William (1995), 'Introduction: In search of nature,' in William Cronon (ed), *Uncommon Ground: Toward Reinventing Nature*, New York: W.W. Norton.

Galbraith, John Kenneth (1973), 'Power and the useful economist,' *American Economic Review*, 63 (1): pp. 1–11.

Hardin, Garrett (1968), 'The tragedy of the commons,' *Science*, 168 (13 December).

Kahn, E. (1985), *The Staffs of Life*, Boston, MA: Little, Brown.

Lukes, Steven (1974), *Power: A Radical View*, London: Macmillan.

Nash, Roderick F. (1990), *The Rights of Nature: A History of Environmental Ethics*, Madison, WI: University of Wisconsin Press.

Ostrom, Elinor (1990), *Governing the Commons: The Evolution of Institutions for Collective Action*, Cambridge: Cambridge University Press.

Pastor, Manuel (2001), 'Building social capital to protect natural capital: the quest for environmental justice,' Working Paper DPE-01-02, Amherst, MA: Political Economy Research Institute, January.

Peña, Devon (2001), 'Rewarding investment in natural capital: the *acequia* commonwealth of the Upper Rio Grande,' in James K. Boyce and Barry Shelley (eds), *Natural Assets: Democratizing Environmental Ownership*, forthcoming.

2. Let them eat risk?

We hold these truths to be self-evident, that all men are created equal, that they are endowed by their Creator with certain unalienable Rights, that among these are Life, Liberty and the pursuit of Happiness.

United States Declaration of Independence, July 4, 1776

Every person shall have the right to an environment which is not detrimental to his or her health or well-being.

Constitution of the Republic of South Africa, April 27, 1994

INTRODUCTION

Two centuries of history separate the United States Declaration of Independence from the post-apartheid Constitution of the Republic of South Africa, but both documents share the fundamental principle that each person has an equal right to life. This remains a revolutionary idea even today, as we enter the twenty-first century.

Bold words do not translate instantly into facts on the ground. More than eight decades elapsed after the Declaration of Independence before the abolition of slavery in the United States. But declarations of principle can define a society's goals, setting a standard by which to judge its subsequent accomplishments.

The idea that every person is endowed with equal rights to life, liberty, the pursuit of happiness, and a safe and healthy environment is a universalistic ethical precept. To be sure, it is not universally accepted, let alone universally honored. But this principle has won increasingly widespread acceptance throughout the world, and today it is formally incorporated in the constitutions of governments that span the globe (for examples, see the accompanying box on the following page).

We find a similar trend towards the assertion of an egalitarian right to a safe environment in judicial interpretations of constitutional guarantees. The Supreme Court of India declared in 1991, for example, that the 'right to life' guaranteed in the Indian Constitution 'includes the right to enjoyment of pollution-free water and air for full enjoyment of life.'[1] Similarly, the Supreme Court of Pakistan has ruled that that country's constitutional right to life includes the right to a clean environment; applying this principle, the

All residents enjoy the right to a healthy, balanced environment.
Argentina Constitution, article 41

Every person shall have the right to a wholesome environment.
Belarus Constitution, article 46

Every person has the right to a healthy, satisfying, and lasting environment.
Benin Constitution, article 27

Citizens have the right to a healthy and favorable environment.
Bulgaria Constitution, article 55

The right to a healthy environment shall be recognized.
Burkina Faso Constitution, article 31

The Constitution guarantees to all persons: ... The right to live in an environment free from contamination.
Chile Constitution (1980), Chapter III, article 19(8)

Every individual has the right to enjoy a healthy environment.
Colombia Constitution, article 79

All persons have the right to a clean and healthy environment.
Ethiopia Constitution, article 44(1)

All citizens shall have the right to a healthy and pleasant environment.
Korea Constitution (1987), Chapter II, article 35

Citizens of the Kyrghyz Republic shall have the right to a healthy, safe environment.
Kyrghyz Constitution, article 35

Every human being has the right to live in an environment that is ecologically safe for life and health.
Moldova Constitution, article 37

Everyone shall have the right to a healthy and ecologically balanced human environment and the duty to defend it.
Portugal Constitution (1982), article 66(1)

Everyone has the right to live in a healthy, balanced environment.
Turkey Constitution (1982), Chapter VIII(A), article 56

Source: Popovic (1996).

Pakistani high court ruled that the dumping of nuclear waste in coastal areas of Pakistan would violate the right to life (Popovic, 1996: nn. 116 and 117).[2]

PUBLIC BADS AND GOODS

Vulnerability to natural and technological disasters is to a large extent a public bad: such disasters typically strike communities, not isolated individuals. By the same token, measures to reduce vulnerability are, to a large extent, public goods.

Disaster-vulnerability reduction is seldom a pure public good, however, in the strict sense of a good which when provided to one is provided to all (non-excludability), and whose consumption by one does not diminish its availability to others (non-rivalness). The twentieth century textbook case of a pure public good was national defense; the twenty-first century textbook case may be policies to combat global warming.

Many measures to reduce disaster vulnerability are impure public goods, which when provided to one are provided to others, but not equally provided to all. For example, flood-control projects provide location-specific benefits, restricted to the subset of the population who live or own assets in the protected area. Similarly, the reinforcement of public infrastructure against earthquakes primarily benefits its users. Safety measures to prevent or contain the effects of industrial accidents primarily benefit those persons who live and work nearby. By virtue of where they live, work, or own property, some members of society are excluded from the benefits of these investments.

Although disaster-vulnerability reduction is not a pure public good, neither is it a pure private good. 'To say a thing is not located at the South Pole,' Paul Samuelson (1955: 356) once remarked, 'does not logically place it at the North Pole.' Measures to reduce disaster vulnerability often lie in intermediate terrain between the two types of goods. Some measures, such as cyclone early-warning systems, are near the public end of the spectrum (although some people – those with radios, for example – are better able to access this information than others). Others, such as the retrofitting of individual homes in seismic zones, are near the private end of the spectrum. Many are somewhere in between.

This means that, in addition to the public policy question of how much disaster-vulnerability reduction to provide, we must face the question of to whom it should be provided. We face not only the classic economic problem of the allocation of scarce resources among competing ends, but also the classic political-economy problem of the allocation of scarce resources among competing individuals, groups, and classes.

Here the focus is on the latter issue. The 'to whom' question is relevant to two key arenas of public policies for risk reduction: first, the allocation of public-sector investment; and second, the creation of an appropriate incentive structure for private-sector investments. In formulating policies in both arenas, two broad classes of approaches to the interpersonal allocation question can be distinguished, which I will call the wealth-based approach and the rights-based approach.

THE WEALTH-BASED APPROACH

The wealth-based approach is so widespread among economists that I might be tempted to call it 'the economic approach,' but for the fact that there are some economists, myself included, who are not enamoured of it. This approach is founded on willingness to pay, which is conditioned, as always, by ability to pay. In brief, the wealth-based approach holds that the interpersonal allocation of disaster-vulnerability reduction should be guided by willingness to pay for those reductions: those individuals who are willing (and, perforce, able) to pay more, deserve to get more. Putting aside interpersonal differences in preferences, including differences in risk aversion, this willingness-to-pay criterion is strongly correlated with wealth. Richer individuals, groups, and classes will get more of the impure public good of disaster-vulnerability reduction than their poorer counterparts.

Whatever its prescriptive appeal, this principle serves rather well as a first approximation of what often happens in practice: it has considerable descriptive relevance. For example, the casualties from the 1976 earthquake in Guatemala were so unevenly distributed across the population – with most of the 22,000 deaths among the poor – that the disaster was dubbed a 'classquake' (Blaikie *et al.*, 1994: 170–1). The earthquake's disproportionate impact on the poor was both due to the location of their homes in landslide-susceptible ravines and gorges, and because they were unable to afford earthquake-resistant construction.

Similarly, the International Federation of the Red Cross secretary-general Didier Cherpitel reminds us that malaria today kills more than 1 million people each year – the equivalent of a Guatemalan earthquake every eight days – mostly in sub-Saharan Africa. The medical capability to avert many, if not all, of these deaths exists, but it is not being used because 'there is no market in malaria and little buying power in Africa' (Cherpitel, 2000).

The wealth-based approach is not confined to the realm of 'what is.' It also exerts a powerful influence, implicitly or explicitly, on many policy makers' notions of 'what ought to be.' One famous (or infamous) example is the 1992 memorandum written by then World Bank chief economist Lawrence Summers, in which he posed the question: 'Just between you and me, shouldn't the World Bank be encouraging more migration of the dirty industries to the LDCs [less developed countries]?'[3] One reason for such a policy, Summers wrote, was that:

> The measurement of the costs of health-impairing pollution depends on the for-gone earnings from increased morbidity and mortality. From this point of view a given amount of health-impairing pollution should be done in the country with the lowest cost, which will be the country with the lowest wages. I think the economic logic of dumping a load of toxic waste in the lowest-wage country is impeccable and we should face up to that.

Summers's memorandum was noteworthy not so much for the view ex-pressed, but for the fact that it was expressed overtly. One virtue of tactlessness is that it spotlights matters which polite society prefers to leave unmentioned.

Interpersonal Weights in the Measurement of Social Welfare

Lest we cede the 'economic' terrain to this particular view, we should recall that other economists have advanced alternative notions of social welfare – and hence of development and efficiency – including several economists who, like Summers, have held prominent positions at the World Bank. A quarter-century ago, for example, in the landmark volume *Redistribution with Growth*, Montek Ahluwalia and Hollis Chenery (1974) defined the growth of social welfare as a weighted sum of the change in welfare of different subsets of the population:

$$G = w_1 g_1 + w_2 g_2 + \ldots + w_n g_n$$

where:

G = index of growth of total social welfare;

g_i = income growth rate of the ith group (for example, quintiles ranked from poorest to richest); and

w_i = welfare weight assigned to the ith group ($\sum_i w_i = 1$).

The authors then distinguished three alternative measures. The first equates the weights, w_i, to each group's share in national income. In a 'typical' developing country, for example, Ahluwalia and Chenery noted that the weight of the poorest quintile would be 0.05, while that of the richest quintile would be 0.53. In other words, the change in welfare of the richest quintile 'counts' over ten times more than that of the poorest, reflecting their respective in-come shares. The resulting index of social welfare is, of course, GNP growth, the conventional measure of economic performance.

Ahluwalia and Chenery's second measure, based on 'equal weights', counts a 1 percent gain in income the same whether it is experienced by the poor or the rich. That is, instead of treating each dollar equally, as in the GNP-weights scheme, the equal-weights scheme treats each person (or income class) equally: $w_1 = w_2 = \ldots = w_n$ for all i groups.

The third measure is based on 'poverty weights.' These are the opposite of the GNP weighting scheme, in that they put greater weight on gains to the poor than on gains to the rich: $w_1 > w_2 > \ldots > w_n$. To illustrate, Ahluwalia and Chenery (1974: 51) suggest poverty weights of 0.6 on the income change of the poorest 40 percent of the population, and 0.1 on that of the richest 20 percent.[4]

Applying these alternative social welfare measures to disaster-risk mitigation (instead of to income), we could put equal weight on risk-reductions to all individuals, regardless of their income or wealth. Or we could put greater weight on risk reductions for the poorest stratum of the population, those who are currently at greatest risk.

THE RIGHTS-BASED APPROACH

This leads back to the rights-based approach. This approach is founded not on the inegalitarian distribution of wealth within and among countries (translated, via real-world markets or the shadow markets of benefit-cost analysis, into willingness to pay), but rather on the egalitarian distribution of the right to a clean and safe environment.

In the allocation of public-sector investments for disaster-risk mitigation, a rights-based approach would assign equal weight to mortality and morbidity impacts across the population, regardless of an individual's wealth or social status. Extending this approach to intergenerational allocation would imply that future lives and health should not be discounted, but rather valued equally with present lives and health.

In shaping private-sector incentives via the legal and regulatory structure, a rights-based approach would define liability on the same basis, with the right to a safe environment held equally by all. Infringements of this right would constitute legal grounds for claims for restitution. Private firms would seek to insure against such claims, opening an avenue for the insurance sector to play a role in the enforcement of safety standards: the more unsafe the facility, the higher the price of insurance. In the case of industrial disasters, at least, this would allow the insurance sector to play a constructive role even when the individuals whose safety is at risk are too poor to buy insurance, for it would be the responsibility of those whose actions jeopardize their safety to insure against any risks to lives and health.

Those of us who sympathize with the rights-based approach are encouraged by the signs of its growing embrace by peoples and governments around the world. But I want to conclude by noting three tensions that confront efforts to apply this approach.

First is the problem posed by non-uniform spatial distribution of human populations. There is a difference between saying that each individual has an equal right to risk mitigation and saying that the weight on each individual's risk should be equal. In the latter case, risks in more densely populated areas carry greater weight than the same risks in less densely populated areas, simply because there are more people to 'add up.' Even the most ardent proponents of the former principle – which aims for equality of risk regardless of where people happen to live – probably would not advocate putting a high-level nuclear waste storage facility in New York City, even if Manhattan Island had the same geological properties as Nevada's Yucca Mountain. But the ethical argument that people should not suffer greater disaster risks simply by virtue of living in less-populated areas cannot be dismissed lightly.

Second is the problem posed by private risk mitigation. As an impure public good, disaster-risk mitigation has some components that can be privately purchased, the distribution of which is founded on ability and willingness to pay – for example, living in more earthquake-resistant homes. This fact provides compelling grounds for public policies which put priority on risk mitigation for those who are less able to obtain it privately – a disaster-vulnerability application of Ahluwalia and Chenery's poverty weights.

Finally, we must face the tensions between an egalitarian allocation of the right to life (and hence to disaster-vulnerability reduction) and the inegalitarian allocation of economic wealth and political power. Lawrence Summers alluded to this problem in his memorandum:

> The problem with the arguments against all of these proposals for more pollution in LDCs (intrinsic rights to certain goods, moral reasons, social concerns, lack of adequate markets, etc.) could be turned around and used more or less effectively against every [World] Bank proposal for liberalization.

This is, perhaps, an exaggeration. Wealth-based and rights-based approaches to interpersonal allocations have long co-existed, and tensions between them will remain a feature of modern societies for the foreseeable future. Nevertheless, the sphere of the rights-based approach has gradually widened over time. The abolition of slavery is one example; the extension of the right to vote to all adult citizens, instead of its restriction on the basis of property ownership, race, or gender, is another; the advent and spread of free public education is a third. The rights-based approach to disaster vulnerability represents a further step on this road.

The radically egalitarian principles proclaimed in the US Declaration of Independence and the South African constitution were, and remain today, actively contested. Yet these principles are on the ascendancy worldwide. As my late countryman, Dr Martin Luther King, Jr (1965) once remarked, 'The arc of the moral universe is long, but it bends toward justice.'

There is no magic recipe for pursuing a rights-based approach to disaster-vulnerability reduction in the face of the predictable opposition from vested interests who favor a wealth-based approach. But those who accept the challenges of moving in this direction can take heart from the belief that history is on their side.

NOTES

This chapter is based on remarks at the ProVention Consortium Conference on Reducing Disasters through Development, Washington, DC, 2–4 February 2000. I am grateful to the conference participants for their thoughts and comments.

1. *Subash Kumar* v. *State of Bihar*, 1991 A.I.R. 420, 424 (India Sup. Ct. 1991), cited by Popovic (1996: n. 118). For discussion, see also Anderson (1996).
2. For discussion, see also Lau (1996).
3. Excerpts of the Summers memorandum were published in *The Economist* (1992: 66).
4. Benefit-cost analysis similarly can incorporate distributional weights that value dollars differently depending on to whom they accrue. For discussions, see Little and Mirrlees (1974: 234–42) and Ray (1984: 22–31).

REFERENCES

Ahluwalia, M.S. and Chenery, H. (1974), 'The economic framework,' in H. Chenery, M.S. Ahluwalia, C.L.G. Bell, J.H. Duloy and R. Jolly (eds), *Redistribution with Growth*, Oxford: Oxford University Press, pp. 38–51.
Anderson, M.R. (1996), 'Individual rights to environmental protection in India,' in A.E. Boyle and Anderson, M.R. (eds), *Human Rights Approaches to Environmental Protection*, Oxford: Clarendon Press, pp. 199–225.
Blaikie, P., Cannon, T., Davis, I. and Wisner, B. (1994), *At Risk: Natural Hazards, People's Vulnerability, and Disasters*, London: Routledge.
Cherpitel, D.J. (2000), 'The changing nature of disaster response and recovery in the 21st century,' statement to the ProVention Consortium Conference on Reducing Disasters through Development, Washington, DC, 2–4 February. Geneva: International Federation of Red Cross and Red Crescent Societies.
Economist, The (1992), 'Let them eat pollution,' 8 February: 66.
King, M.L. Jr. (1965), 'Remaining awake through a great revolution', commencement address for Oberlin College, Oberlin, Ohio, June.
Lau, M. (1996), 'Islam and judicial activism: public interest litigation and environmental protection in the Islamic Republic of Pakistan,' in A.E. Boyle and M.R. Anderson (eds), *Human Rights Approaches to Environmental Protection*, Oxford: Clarendon Press, pp. 285–302.

Little, I.M.D. and Mirrlees, J. (1974), *Project Appraisal and Planning for Developing Countries*, New York: Basic Books.

Popovic, N.A.F. (1996), 'In pursuit of environmental human rights,' *Columbia Human Rights Law Review*, 27: 487–620.

Ray, A. (1984), *Cost-benefit Analysis: Issues and Methodologies*, Baltimore, MD: Johns Hopkins University Press, for World Bank.

Samuelson, P. (1955), 'Diagrammatic exposition of a theory of public expenditure,' *Review of Economics and Statistics*, 37(4): 350–6.

3.   Investing in natural and human capital

(with Olman Segura Bonilla)

INTRODUCTION

Until recently, economics and ecology were treated as distinct and unrelated subjects. But today the recognition is growing that the ways human beings manage nature are closely related to the ways we manage relationships among ourselves.

Threats to the ecosystems that underpin economic activity are forcing us to reconsider our treatment of natural resources in our daily lives and in our fields of study. The assumption that technical progress is a perfect substitute for natural resources is losing credibility. The inadequacy of myopic time horizons in the face of long-term environmental degradation is becoming ever more apparent. These insights have given impetus to the idea of sustainable development.

The treatment of natural resources as natural capital is an important element of the new sustainable development economics. Natural resources can no longer be regarded as free goods. In microeconomic decisions and in national accounts, the depletion of the natural resource base must be treated as a cost. At the same time, it is possible to invest in natural capital, for example via reforestation, soil restoration, and pollution control. In other words, some natural capital can be, if not 'man-made,' at least helped along by purposeful human endeavor.

This chapter considers the prospects for sustainable development in the so-called Third World (that is, in the agrarian and semi-industrialized economies of Asia, Africa, and Latin America). We argue that a necessary condition for sustainable development in these countries is a radical improvement in the nutritional well-being, health, and education of their poor majorities. In other words, investment in natural capital requires investment in human capital.

ECONOMIC MODELS

Classical economics distinguished three factors of production: land, labor, and capital. Today the terms 'natural capital,' 'human capital,' and 'man-made capital' have replaced the original triad. Natural capital, like other forms of capital, can depreciate. Economic models and economic policies long ignored this basic fact, but in recent years it has gained recognition. It has been estimated, for example, that the air and water pollution controls implemented in the United States in the 1970s caused the country's measured GNP to be 5 percent lower in 1990 than it would have been without the controls (Koop 1992). This cost represents a form of investment in natural capital.

The economic models applied in Third World countries in the name of development have typically neglected environmental concerns. The import-substitution model developed after World War Two had important negative environmental impacts (Segura 1992). Selective trade barriers built indus-trial sectors highly dependent on imported capital goods and petroleum. Industrial concentration in urban centers contributed to multiple environ-mental ills. In agriculture, the 'green revolution' technology increased yields of food grains, but at the cost of intensive use of agrochemicals and losses of genetic diversity.

More recently, an outward-oriented model of development has become fashionable. In some regions, such as Central America, this model empha-sizes exports of non-traditional agricultural products; in others, such as Southeast Asia, it emphasizes exports of manufactured goods. The new ex-port-led model typically calls for less state intervention in the economy, taking it to be virtually synonymous with inefficiency, and instead embraces open markets, international trade, and comparative advantage. Like the im-port-substitution model before it, however, this model does not consider the social costs of natural resource depletion. The correct allocation of natural resources, as of other commodities, is simply left to the market (Stanfield 1991). Since market prices generally fail to capture the full cost of deprecia-tion of natural capital, the spontaneous action of markets cannot be expected to lead to sustainability (Daly 1991; Kaimowitz 1992).

A central tenet of the new ecological economics is the proposition that, far from being a perfect substitute for natural capital, investment in man-made capital requires natural capital (Pearce *et al.* 1990; Daly 1991). This chapter advances an analogous thesis: investment in natural capital requires human capital. Specifically, we believe that dramatic improvements in the nutritional well-being, health, and education of the poor majority in the Third World are crucial to the goal of sustainable development. The linkage between human capital and natural capital has far-reaching implications, for it means that issues of the distribution of wealth and power are fundamental to the quest for sustainable development.

A TYPOLOGY OF ENVIRONMENTAL DEGRADATION

A common feature in diverse strands of economic theory in the latter half of the twentieth century has been the tendency to downplay the importance of distributional issues. Neoclassical economics focuses on the goal of efficiency – defined in Paretian terms as a situation in which no one can be made better off without making someone else worse off. The division of the economic pie is left to politicians and others uninhibited by the neoclassical economists' professed aversion to 'value judgments.'

Development economics has focused on the goal of economic growth – defined as rising gross national product. In the 1970s, in response to the perceived failure of the benefits of growth to 'trickle down' to the poor, mainstream development economics embraced the goal of 'redistribution with growth,' but this meant merely an effort to secure a more equitable distribution of new increments to national income, rather than a redistribution of the existing pie (Chenery *et al.* 1974).

While economists tend to downplay distribution, ecologists tend to ignore it altogether. This is not surprising, since social differentiation is generally absent in the non-human populations studied by ecologists. Consider, for example, aquatic weeds growing in a pond. If volume doubles every day, and the weeds fill the entire pond in 30 days, the pond will, of course, be half-full on the twenty-ninth day. Ecologists have used this example to illustrate the perils of exponential growth of human population (Ehrlich and Ehrlich 1990: 15–16). A notable feature of this metaphor is the total absence of distribution as an issue. Pond weeds are not differentiated by wealth or power. Hence neither the pond weeds' rate of nutrient depletion nor their rate of growth is affected by differences between rich and poor, or powerful and powerless. Moreover, the symptoms of ecological stress will affect equally all the weeds in the pond.

By contrast, inequalities of wealth and power are a noteworthy feature of human societies. These inequalities are of crucial importance in understanding the causes and consequences of environmental degradation. Why do people engage in economic activities which degrade the environment? And why, if they choose to do so, should anyone else worry about it? The answer to the first question, of course, is that some people reap net benefits from the activities, or at least think that they do. The answer to the second is that other people bear net costs as a result of these same activities. Leaving aside for the moment the possibility of ignorance (when people think that they will reap net benefits, but really will bear net costs), the winners and losers are different people.

In analyzing the causes and consequences of environmental degradation, therefore, one can pose three further questions:

- Who reaps the benefits?
- Who bears the costs?
- Why are the winners able to impose costs on the losers?

In neoclassical environmental economics, these questions are resolutely pushed aside. Negative externalities result from impersonal market failures; distribution has no bearing on their causes. As to consequences, neoclassical environmental economics attempts to sidestep distributional value judgments by means of the 'compensation test': could the winners, in theory, compensate the losers, and remain better off? As Sen (1987: 33) observes, however, even by the Pareto-efficiency criterion, this device is either unconvincing (if compensation is not in fact paid) or redundant (if it is).

As a step towards redressing this neglect of distributional issues, Figure 3.1 shows a simple four-fold classification of environmental degradation, based on the relative wealth positions of the winners and losers. In Type I environmental degradation, both winners and losers are rich. In Type II, the rich bear the costs of environmental degradation caused by the poor. In Type III the reverse occurs: the poor bear the costs of environmental degradation caused by the rich. Finally, in Type IV the poor are both winners and losers.

Winners

		Rich	Poor
Losers	Rich	I	II
	Poor	III	IV

Figure 3.1   A typology of environmental degradation

A few examples will illustrate these possibilities. If a rich homeowner instructs his gardener to burn yard waste in the back yard, and the smoke pollutes the air breathed by his affluent neighbors, this is Type I environmental degradation. If a poor person tosses a bag of refuse on the rich person's lawn, this is Type II. If the rich person sends his trash to a landfill or incinerator that pollutes an adjacent community inhabited by poor people, this is Type III. And if a poor person burns his trash in a metal drum behind his dwelling, polluting the air breathed by his comparably poor neighbors, this is Type IV.

The relative frequency and importance of these four types of environmental degradation – with society appropriately partitioned into rich and poor – is an interesting topic for research. As a preliminary hypothesis, we offer the following: Type III environmental degradation is more prevalent than Types I and IV, and these in turn, are more prevalent than Type II. The rich are thus better able to impose environmental costs on the poor than vice-versa.

There are several reasons to expect this to be true. First, since environmental degradation is, *ceteris paribus*, an increasing function of consumption and production, the fact that the rich consume more implies that they generate more environmental degradation. Second, since money can be spent to reduce or avoid bearing the costs of pollution, for example by residing and vacationing in relatively uncontaminated ecosystems, the rich can more readily escape the costs of environmental degradation. Finally, wealth is positively correlated with power, and power increases one's ability to impose negative externalities on others and to resist having them imposed on oneself (see Chapter 4).

HUMAN CAPITAL AND NATURAL CAPITAL

We now turn to the linkages between human capital and natural capital. We discuss these under four headings: time horizons, power, knowledge, and population growth.

Time Horizons

People cannot be expected to cease activities that degrade the environment yet are essential to the sustenance of their families. Immediate survival is the paramount objective. In the countryside, many of the poor are driven to cultivate fragile environments – steep hillsides, semi-arid lands, thin tropical forest soils – where erosion and nutrient depletion follow swiftly. In the cities, they often live and work in highly precarious and contaminated environments. These choices are the results of desperation, which compels the poor to reap small immediate gains even at the price of large future costs.

The poor themselves are often all too well aware of the damaging long-run consequences of their activities. But to see tomorrow, one must survive today. The end result can be a vicious circle, in which poverty accelerates the depreciation of natural capital, which leads in turn to further impoverishment (Durning 1989; World Bank 1992). In terms of our categories in Figure 3.1, this is Type IV environmental degradation.

By lessening their desperation, improvements in nutrition, health, and education of the poor would permit them to invest more in natural capital: to protect and improve the physical environments, both rural and urban, which are essential to their own long-run well-being. In effect, human capital investments can lengthen the time horizons of the poor.

Power

Investments in the human capital of the poor can also strengthen their ability to combat environmental degradation of which they are victims, not perpetrators – Type III environmental degradation in Figure 3.1. This is potentially the most important linkage between human capital and natural capital, for much of the pollution and natural resource depletion in the developing countries, as elsewhere, is driven not by the desperation of the poor, but by the greed and negligence of the rich.

Tropical deforestation illustrates this point. In Central America, where very rapid deforestation took place in the 1960s and 1970s, the main cause was the clearing of lands for cattle ranching, stimulated by favorable access to subsidized credit and to the protected US beef market. The main beneficiaries of this privately profitable (but socially costly) process were the large *hacenderos* and owners of meat packing plants, both exemplified by former Nicaraguan dictator Anastasio Somoza. The main losers were poor peasants, who were denied access to previously cultivated as well as forested lands, and for whom extensive cattle grazing provided meager employment opportunities (Edelman 1985; Williams 1986; Ascher and Healy 1990).

In Southeast Asia, the main cause of rapid deforestation has been logging for tropical hardwood exports. The main beneficiaries are logging concessionaires – who are often military officers and the political cronies of top government officials – who capture rights to cut the public forests as a form of political patronage. Once again, the main losers are the poor, including displaced forest dwellers (often ethnic minorities) and downstream peasants whose crops depend on the forest's hydrological 'sponge effect' (Repetto and Gillis 1988; Hurst 1990; Kummer 1992; Boyce 1993).

In the Brazilian Amazon, the driving forces and main beneficiaries of deforestation have been generals, land speculators, and large-scale cattle ranchers. The principal victims are the 200,000 indigenous people of the Amazon, and the 2 million other Brazilians who earn their living by gathering rubber, nuts, resins, palm products, and medicines from the forest (Guppy 1984; Hecht and Cockburn 1990).

Third World elites have not pursued these assaults on the world's tropical forests on their own. On the one hand, they have many times enjoyed avid support – economic, political, and military – from the governments and international financial institutions of the industrialized countries. On the other hand, they often employ their poorer countrymen to do the hard work. In Costa Rica, for example, landless farmers are often contracted to clear the land in return for permission to grow crops on it for two or three years, after which the cattle rancher converts it to pasture (Edelman 1985). In Brazil, temporary laborers, sometimes including indigenous people, are hired at minimal wages to cut and bum the forest. But as Barraclough and Ghimire (1990: 13) remark: 'To blame poor migrants for destroying the forest is like blaming poor conscripts for the ravages of war.'

Investment in the human capital of the poor can increase their leverage to oppose such instances of Type III environmental degradation. With better nutrition, health, and education, the poor become better able to resist the economic and political pressures of the rich; better able to analyze the causes and consequences of environmental degradation; and better able to score victories in the political arenas where conflicts are ultimately resolved. The complementarity between human capital and natural capital is here mediated by what can be termed the 'political capital' of the poor.

Knowledge

Knowledge of the environment is itself a form of human capital. While it would be quite erroneous to assume that the poor are entirely ignorant of their environment – on the contrary, they are frequently more knowledgeable about environmental matters than the rich – it would be equally erroneous to assume romantically that their environmental knowledge is so profound as to be incapable of further advance. Environmental education can be particularly important in situations where people confront new environments, or where they face radically new stresses in old ones.

By improving natural resource management by the poor, education can help to reduce Type IV and Type II environmental degradation. No less important, education can enhance their ability to contest Type III environmental degradation. The latter effect comes about for two reasons. First, education can improve knowledge of environmental costs whose impacts and sources otherwise remain obscure. It is one thing to know that your child is sick, but something else to trace that sickness to a specific source of environmental contamination. Second, education can improve knowledge of how to wage successful political struggles: how to lobby government officials, initiate legal actions, and mobilize public opinion.

In sum, by providing environmental knowledge to people who have an incentive to use it, education can alter the balance of power and thereby tilt environmental outcomes towards greater protection of natural capital.

Population Growth

In our view the impact of population growth upon natural capital is more complex than is often assumed. Obviously, the number of human beings on our planet cannot grow forever. It is equally obvious that, holding any variable per capita constant, more people means more of that variable. These truisms, however, do not logically imply the proposition that at this moment in human history the world is overpopulated, nor that population growth is today the principal cause of worldwide environmental degradation.

Consider the simple formula advanced by Ehrlich and Holdren (1971):

$$I = P \times F$$

where I = the total negative impact on the environment; P = population; and F = per capita negative impact on the environment. This mathematical identity is often taken to prove that population growth necessarily accelerates environmental degradation. Let us define I_n as that subset of environmental degradation which has no causal relation whatsoever with population growth. An example might be the environmental degradation caused by the manufacture, deployment, and disposal of weapons for the United States military, which reportedly generates more toxic waste every year than the world's five largest multinational chemical companies combined (Seager 1993). Let I_p represent that subset of environmental degradation which is causally related to population growth. Let F_n and F_p represent these two subsets per capita. Now we can write the identity $I_n = P \times F_n$: total non-population-related negative environmental impact equals population multiplied by such impact per capita. Yet it would be utterly fallacious to conclude, on the basis of this formula, that population growth is a driving force behind contamination of the environment by the US military.

This is not to argue that population growth has no environmental effects. The point is that the formula, $I = P \times F$, tells us nothing about the importance of population growth as a cause of environmental degradation. That is, it tells us nothing about the magnitudes of the ratios I_n/I and I_p/I. The formula would be equally correct no matter whether $I_n/I = 1$ (and population growth had no effect whatsoever on environmental degradation), or $I_n/I = 0$ (and all environmental degradation was inexorably multiplied by population growth), or anything in between. In other words, the formula is an empty tautology.

Part of the appeal of this defective analysis, especially among natural scientists, may lie in the analogy it makes between humans and other animals. An increase in caterpillars, for instance, means more leaves must be eaten if they are to survive and reproduce. In the absence of predators or pesticides, their numbers will grow until famine or disease precipitates a population crash. Unlike animals that merely consume, however, people both produce and consume. To characterize babies born in Bangladesh, the Philippines, or elsewhere as 'mouths' (Ehrlich and Ehrlich 1990: 72, 75) is to ignore their brains and hands. Animals cannot invest in natural capital. Humans can.

Improvements in the human capital of the poor majority, notably in health and education, historically have been associated with declining fertility for a number of reasons: women gain greater access to employment opportunities outside the home; lower infant and child mortality means fewer births are needed to attain a given probability of survival to adulthood; the importance of children's labor in family income diminishes; access to birth control and supporting health services improves; and so on (Cassen 1976; Repetto 1979; Caldwell 1982). Insofar as population growth exacerbates environmental degradation – and there are undoubtedly settings where, all else equal, it does so – this demographic transition constitutes a further link between human capital and natural capital.

We have argued above that investment in the human capital of the poor can increase their relative power. The possible effects on birth rates of this shift in the balance of power merits comment. Greater power for the poor – especially for women – increases the political effectiveness of their demand for access to birth control and reproductive health services. By the same token, however, it strengthens their capacity to resist unwanted birth control measures pushed upon them by governments in the name of population control. For example, improvements in living standards in Bangladesh might reduce the number of women who accept sterilization in return for 'incentive' payments in the form of cash and clothing (Hartmann 1987). Empowerment of the poor thus could cause a short-run increase in fertility in settings where population-control incentives and coercion are now in use. However, this would also reduce the risk of a popular backlash against family planning programs, as occurred in India after the coercive sterilization drive of the mid-1970s. At the same time, it would give governments and international agencies greater incentive to provide more 'user-friendly' birth control options, enhancing the long-run prospects for fertility decline.

CONCLUSIONS

In this chapter we have presented a case for investment in human capital as a necessary condition for investment in natural capital in the developing countries. Improvements in the nutrition, health, and education of the poor majority would lengthen their time horizons, strengthen their power to oppose environmental degradation caused by others, enhance their knowledge of environmental costs and how to reduce them, and contribute to voluntary diminution of population growth.

The foregoing analysis implies a dual role for the state. On the one hand, state interventions are needed to correct market failures; for example, through regulations on the use of toxic chemicals, incentives for reforestation, taxes on pollution, and depletion quotas for non-renewable resources. On the other hand, the state can directly and indirectly promote investment in the human capital of the poor.

Today we find a contradictory policy in place in many developing countries. In the name of macroeconomic adjustment, governments are slashing social expenditure, cutting public investment, and tightening credit. Although reductions in public expenditure are often unavoidable, it is important to establish priorities. Policies should be avoided which increase poverty, adversely affect public health, undermine the state's capability for environmental protection, or reduce financing for the development and diffusion of more environmentally sound technologies.

Many serious threats to sustainability in the Third World originate elsewhere, in the industrialized countries. In the case of carbon dioxide emissions, for example, per capita output from industrial processes in the United States is 19.7 metric tonnes per year, compared to 0.9 tonne for the average Costa Rican, or 0.1 for the average Bangladeshi (World Resources Institute 1992). In addition to the industrialized countries' role in global environmental threats, their trade and financial policies often operate to the detriment of both the economic and environmental well-being of the poor majority in the Third World.

In the industrialized countries as well as the developing countries, therefore, complementary investments in natural capital and the human capital of the poor will require profound institutional changes. If sustainable development is to be more than a passing slogan, it will demand a reshaping not only of human relationships with nature, but also of our relationships with each other. This is the great challenge facing not only economists and ecologists, but humankind as a whole.

REFERENCES

Ascher, W. and Healy, R. (1990), *Natural Resource Policymaking in Developing Countries*, Durham, NC, and London: Duke University Press.

Barraclough, S. and Ghimire, K. (1990), 'The social dynamics of deforestation in developing countries,' Discussion Paper no. 16, Geneva: United Nations Research Institute for Social Development.

Boyce, J.K. (1993), *The Philippines: The Political Economy of Growth and Impover-*

ishment in the Marcos Era, London: Macmillan; Honolulu: University of Hawaii Press; and Quezon City: Ateneo de Manila University Press.

Caldwell, J. (1982), *The Theory of Fertility Decline*, New York: Academic Press.

Cassen, R.H. (1976), 'Population and development: A survey,' *World Development*, 4 (10/11): 785–830.

Chenery, H., Ahluwalia, M.S., Bell, C.L.G., Duloy, J.H. and Jolly, R. (1974), *Redistribution with Growth*, Oxford: Oxford University Press.

Daly, H. (1991), *Steady-state Economics*, 2nd edn, Washington, DC: Island Press.

Durning, A.B. (1989), 'Poverty and the environment: Reversing the downward spiral,' Worldwatch Paper no. 92, November, Washington, DC: Worldwatch Institute.

Economist, The (1992), 'Let them eat pollution,' 8 February: 66.

Edelman, M. (1985), 'Land and labor in an expanding economy: Agrarian capitalism and the hacienda system in Guanacaste Province, Costa Rica,' PhD dissertation, Columbia University.

Ehrlich, P. and Ehrlich, A. (1990), *The Population Explosion*, New York: Simon & Schuster.

Ehrlich, P. and Holdren, J. (1971), 'The impact of population growth,' *Science*, 171 (26 March): 1212–7.

Guppy, N. (1984), 'Tropical deforestation: A global view,' *Foreign Affairs*, 62 (4): 928–65.

Hartmann, B. (1987), *Reproductive Rights and Wrongs: The Global Politics of Population Control and Contraceptive Choice*, New York: Harper & Row.

Hecht, S. and Cockburn, A. (1990), *The Fate of the Forest: Developers, Destroyers and Defenders of the Amazon*, New York: HarperCollins.

Hurst, P. (1990), *Rainforest Politics: Ecological Destruction in South-East Asia*, London: Zed Books.

Kaimowitz, D. (1992), 'La valorización del futuro: un reto para desarrollo sostenible en América Latina,' in O. Segura (ed), *Desarrollo Sostenible y Políticas Económicas en América Latina*. San José, Costa Rica: Editorial DEI, 119–26.

Koop, R.J. (1992), 'The role of natural assets in economic development,' *Resources*, Winter: 7–10.

Kummer, D.M. (1992), *Deforestation in the Post-War Philippines*, Chicago: University of Chicago Press.

Pearce, D., Barbier, E. and Markandya, A. (1990), *Sustainable Development: Economics and Environment in the Third World*, Aldershot, Hants and Northampton, MA: Edward Elgar.

Repetto, R. (1979), *Economic Equality and Fertility in Developing Countries*, Baltimore, MD: Johns Hopkins University Press.

Repetto, R. and Gillis, M. (eds) (1988), *The Forest for the Trees: Government Policies and the Misuse of Forest Resources*, Cambridge: Cambridge University Press.

Seager, J. (1993), *Earth Follies: Coming to Feminist Terms with the Global Environmental Crisis*, London: Routledge.

Segura, O. (1992), 'El desarrollo sostenible y la liberalización del comercio internacional,' in O. Segura (ed), *Desarrollo Sostenible y Políticas Económicas en América Latina*, San José, Costa Rica: Editorial DEI, 71–6.

Segura, O. (ed) (1992), *Desarrollo Sostenible y Políticas Económicas en América Latina*, San José, Costa Rica: Editorial DEI.

Sen, A.K. (1987), *On Ethics and Economics*, Oxford: Basil Blackwell.

Stanfield, D. (1991), 'La liberalización del comercio international y la agricultura sostenible: el imacto del GATT', paper presented at the conference on Desarrollo

Sostenible, Ecología, Medio Ambiente: Un Reto para el Siglo XXI, organized by the Centro Agrónomo Tropical de Investigación y Enseñanza (CATIE), held in Panama, 27 September.

Williams, R.G. (1986), *Export Agriculture and the Crisis in Central America*, Chapel Hill, NC: University of North Carolina Press.

World Bank (1992), *World Development Report 1992*, New York: Oxford University Press.

World Resources Institute (1992), *World Resources 1992–93*, New York: Oxford University Press.

4. Inequality as a cause of environmental degradation

We can't see how the authorities can say they defend the ecological system, while at the same time deploying police to protect those who are destroying the forest.
Brazilian rubber tappers union leader Chico Mendes (1989:60), shortly before his assassination

INTRODUCTION

Economic activities that degrade the environment generally yield winners and losers. Without winners – people who derive net benefit from the activity, or at least think that they do – the environmentally degrading activities would not occur. Without losers – people who bear net costs – they would not matter in terms of human well-being.[1]

In analyzing an environmentally degrading economic activity, therefore, we can pose three basic questions, as noted in Chapter 3:

- Who are the winners?
- Who are the losers?
- Why are the winners able to impose costs on the losers?

The last question has three possible answers. One is that the losers do not yet exist. They belong to future generations, and so are not here to defend themselves. The second possibility is that the losers already exist, but they do not know it; they lack information about the costs of environmental degradation. The third possibility is that the losers exist and know it, but they lack the power to prevent the winners from imposing costs on them. This chapter addresses mainly, though not exclusively, the last case.[2]

Traditional microeconomic analysis treats the external costs of environmental degradation as an impersonal by-product of economic activity. The identities of those who produce negative externalities, and of those on the receiving end, are irrelevant to both the diagnosis of the problem and the prescription of a solution. One need not ask *who* wins and loses, but only whether the marginal social cost of the activity exceeds its marginal social benefit. If it does, the usual remedies – taxes, regulation, or market creation –

are proffered. Whether these remedies are in fact implemented is the province of political science, not economics.

In this chapter, I propose a political-economy framework for the analysis of environmental degradation, in which the identities of winners and losers matter. I hypothesize that if the winners are relatively powerful and the losers relatively powerless, more environmental degradation will occur than in the reverse situation. These outcomes are guided by what I term a *power-weighted social decision rule*. Furthermore, I hypothesize that, all else equal, greater inequalities of power and wealth lead to more environmental degradation, for three reasons: first, via asymmetries in the power-weighted social decision rule; second, via impacts on valuations of the costs and benefits of environmentally degrading activities; and third, via impacts on the rate of time preference applied to the environment.

THE POWER-WEIGHTED SOCIAL DECISION RULE

Cost-benefit analysis prescribes a precise rule to govern social decisions: an environmentally degrading activity should be pursued as long as its marginal net impact on society is positive. The latter is calculated, in theory, as the sum of marginal benefits and costs to everyone affected, including the external costs of pollution and resource depletion. In practice, this calculation is often quite difficult, but my concern here is not practical difficulties, but the theory itself. It is possible, indeed likely, that not everyone affected by the activity will derive a net benefit. Some will bear net costs. But as long as the winners could in theory compensate the losers, and still win, the activity is deemed socially 'efficient' and it passes the cost-benefit test.

Contrast this prescription to what happens in a theoretical *laissez-faire* world. The costs to the losers are simply ignored by the winners, who pursue the activity as long as it remains privately beneficial for them to do so. Hence the activity is pursued even when its net social impact is negative.

Figure 4.1 depicts these two theoretical cases. The downward-sloping line represents the marginal benefit to the winners, the upward-sloping line the marginal cost to the losers. The benefit curve slopes downward due to diminishing welfare gains (the sum of producers' surplus and consumers' surplus) from additional units of the environmentally degrading activity. The cost curve slopes upward due to the rising marginal impact of additional units of environmental degradation. For example, the environmental cost of clearing the last 1000 acres of a 10,000-hectare rainforest exceeds that of clearing the first 1000. The socially 'efficient' level of environmental degradation prescribed by cost-benefit analysis is D_S.[3] The *laissez-faire* level privately chosen by the winners is D_P.

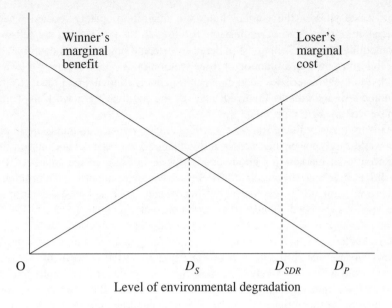

Figure 4.1   Determination of the level of environmental degradation

Real-world outcomes often do not conform to these ideal types. Winners are constrained by reactions of the losers in the form of informal sanctions, private bargaining, or pressure for government intervention. These can limit environmental degradation to a level below D_P. There is, however, no guarantee that the result will be D_S. The reason advanced by Coase (1960) is that transaction costs often prevent the attainment of the social optimum. It is not costless, for example, for the losers to bargain with the winners or to lobby the government.

Here I wish to suggest a further reason for failures to achieve the cost-benefit optimum: Real-world outcomes are shaped by the relative power of the winners and losers. Consider two individuals, A and B, who work in the same office. A enjoys cigars, while B abhors smoke. How much, if at all, will A smoke cigars in the office? If A happens to be the boss and B a secretary, the answer is likely to differ from the reverse situation. More generally, I hypothesize that A's ability to impose external costs on B depends on A's *power* relative to B.

In Coasian terms, we could define power as the ability to bear transaction costs. In the above example, the boss could be said to be better able to bear the 'transaction costs' of setting office smoking policy. Similarly, we can predict that waste-disposal facilities will be sited in the least powerful communities, or, in Coasian terms, in communities whose residents are least able to bear the transaction costs of resisting such facilities. The fact that hazardous-waste sites in the United States are disproportionately located where racial minorities live (Commission for Racial Justice 1987) thus tells us something about the relationship between race and power in that country.

Relative power is a function of three factors: (a) a vector of power-relevant individual characteristics such as wealth, gender, ethnicity, and race; (b) the numbers of individuals involved; and (c) the political framework in which these variables are mapped to power.

In any given political framework, for example, richer individuals are likely to wield more power than poorer individuals. Money speaks not only in the conventional markets for goods and services, but also in the 'markets' for political influence (Ferguson 1983). Similarly, environment-related problems that predominantly or exclusively afflict women, such as breast cancer, may receive less remedial attention than problems that afflict men (Agarwal 1992). The relevance of race and ethnicity has already been suggested.

The extent to which differences in wealth and other individual characteristics translate into differences in power depends on the political framework. Power and wealth are likely to be positively correlated, for example, but the strength of that correlation may vary considerably. Power may be more highly concentrated than wealth, or less so, depending on the political framework. The importance of this framework was vividly illustrated in the former Soviet Union, where a highly inequitable distribution of power prevailed despite a relatively egalitarian distribution of wealth. The result, as one would predict under the power-weighted social decision rule, was large environmental costs imposed above all on people with little power.[4]

If, as is frequently the case, the winners and losers are groups rather than single individuals, their relative power also depends on the numbers involved. A group's power may be simply the sum of the individual power of its members, but this depends on the institutional framework for collective action. Departures from scale-neutrality are conceivable in either direction. If, as Olson (1965) and others have argued, small groups organize more readily than big ones, large numbers are a liability. On the other hand, some institutional frameworks – including simple majority rule – yield strength through numbers.

Returning to Figure 4.1, we can describe real-world outcomes as the result of a *power-weighted social decision rule*. When the losers from environmental degradation are less powerful than the winners, environmental degradation exceeds D_S; when the losers are more powerful than the winners, it is less than D_S. In this framework, the theoretical outcomes under cost-benefit analysis and *laissez-faire* represent special cases: the first corresponds to an equal distribution of power between winners and losers; the second to a situation in which the losers exercise no power whatsoever.

In the same way that the choice-theoretic model of microeconomic theory infers utility from the revealed preferences of the individual, we can infer power from the revealed preferences of society. If, for example, the actual level of environmental degradation is D_{SDR} in Figure 4.1, where the marginal cost to the losers is four times the marginal benefit to the winners, we can conclude that the winners are four times more powerful than the losers.

This definition, like that of utility, is circular: power both explains and is revealed by choice. But circularity need not imply emptiness. Like the utility-maximization model of individual choice, the power-weighted model of social choice yields testable hypotheses. It predicts that social choices governing environmental degradation will consistently favor some people over others, and that this pattern will correlate with other power-related variables. This hypothesis as to the identities of winners and losers – that is, the direction of negative externalities – forms one element in a research agenda in the political economy of environmental degradation.

INEQUALITY AND POWER-WEIGHTED SOCIAL DECISIONS

At first glance, the aggregate effect of power inequality on the level of environmental degradation may seem ambiguous. On the one hand, when the winners are more powerful than the losers the power-weighted social decision rule predicts that greater inequality will lead to more environmental degradation, pushing the outcome further to the right of D_S in Figure 4.1 – in the most extreme case, to D_P.

On the other hand, when the losers are more powerful than the winners, greater power inequality reduces the level of environmental degradation, pushing it further to the left of D_S, and in the most extreme case preventing it altogether. In social cost-benefit terms, the result is a sub-optimal level of environmental degradation. As an example, consider the forcible eviction of slum dwellers, which I witnessed in Dhaka, the capital of Bangladesh, in 1975. At that time shantytowns were bulldozed, and their residents literally thrown into military trucks and deposited at bleak camps far from urban employment and services. The government called this 'beautification.' The benefits to the poor of living in the shantytowns probably outweighed the cost to the rich of glimpsing the squalor from their passing automobiles. But in this instance, power inequality generated what might be termed excessive environmental protection.

The question is whether these two effects can be expected to offset each other, such that power inequality has no predictable net aggregate impact on the level of environmental degradation. I think not, for four reasons.

First, insofar as power correlates positively with wealth, situations in which the winners are powerful can be expected to occur more frequently than situations in which the losers are powerful. The countries with the richest 20 percent of the world's population (in terms of average incomes) receive 83 percent of global income, while the countries with the poorest 60 percent receive only 6 percent (United Nations Development Programme 1992: 36). Similar though less extreme disparities exist within nations. Hence economic activities driven by the consumption demand of the rich account for a far larger share of world output than those driven by the consumption demand of the poor.[5] In economic terms, the rich derive benefit from these activities in the form of consumers' surplus. And, as owners of a disproportionate share of productive assets, the rich capture much of the other component of economic benefits, producers' surplus.[6]

Second, too little environmental degradation can be more readily corrected than too much, due to physical irreversibilities. When a species is extinguished, a non-renewable resource depleted, the soil washed away, or a long-lived pollutant discharged into the environment, the damage cannot be easily undone. Shifts over time in the balance of power can increase suboptimal levels of environmentally degrading activities, but cannot reduce such long-term costs of excessive levels.

Third, the rising marginal cost curve implies that the excess environmental degradation driven by powerful winners is more damaging, in terms of its social costs, than the lower levels prevented by powerful losers. Finally, if we take account of the benefits derived from the environmentally degrading activity as well as its costs, *both* situations – too much environmental degradation and too little – create welfare losses. These losses are additive, not mutually offsetting.

For these reasons, the ability of the powerful to limit environmental degradation by the less powerful cannot be expected to offset the failure of the less powerful to limit environmental degradation by the powerful. The power-weighted social decision rule yields an unambiguous prediction: the greater the inequality of power, the greater the extent and social cost of environmental degradation. This prediction as to magnitudes is a second element for a research agenda in the political economy of environmental degradation.

INEQUALITY AND ENVIRONMENTAL VALUATION

The foregoing positive analysis departs from the normative framework of conventional cost-benefit analysis in one important respect: in social decisions, the distribution of power affects the weights accorded to costs and benefits received by different groups. So far, however, I have not inquired into the monetary valuations of these costs and benefits themselves, nor into how these are affected by inequality. I now turn to these issues.

Monetary valuations in cost-benefit analysis are in theory based on market prices, or more precisely, on the market prices that would prevail in the hypothetical world of a perfectly competitive general equilibrium. These prices have three fundamental determinants, usually taken as exogenous: the initial distribution of endowments, consumer preferences, and technology.

In practice, problems arise from market failure, incomplete information, price distortions and so on. These have generated a voluminous literature, the guiding principle of which remains valuation in terms of willingness to pay. The costs of air pollution, for example, are measured in terms of how much the affected parties would be willing to pay for cleaner air.

Willingness to pay is constrained, of course, by ability to pay. The latter in turn depends on the initial distribution of endowments. In real-world markets and in the shadow markets of cost-benefit analysis, different distributions generate different prices. For example, if wealth is highly concentrated, demand for basic necessities like rice and beans will be less than if wealth is more equitably distributed, and their 'efficient' level of output will consequently be lower. Similarly, the 'efficient' level of air pollution is higher when those who breathe the dirty air are poor than when they are rich, for the simple reason that the poor's ability and willingness to pay to avoid it is lower.[7]

The effect of regressive income redistribution – in the case argued above to be most important, when those who bear the costs of the environmentally degrading activity are poor relative to those who reap its benefits – is depicted in Figure 4.2. The solid lines represent the original marginal valuation curves. The broken lines depict the same curves after a redistribution of income from the poorer losers to the richer winners. The 'efficient' level of environmental degradation increases from D_S to D'_S. The level predicted by the power-weighted social decision rule, while holding the power weights constant, increases from D_{SDR} to D'_{SDR}. If income redistribution is accompanied by similar redistribution of power, then the predicted level of environmental degradation increases still further to D''_{SDR}.

Consider, for example, how an increase in income inequality might affect the conversion of tropical forests to cattle ranches. If the increased purchasing power of relatively rich consumers raises market demand for beef, the 'benefit' from deforestation increases. Meanwhile, as incomes decline for poorer people hurt by conversion – for example, hunter-gatherers living in the forest or small farmers living downstream – so does their ability (and hence willingness) to pay to prevent it. The 'cost' of deforestation falls accordingly. The result, prescribed by cost-benefit analysis and predicted by the power-weighted social decision rule, is more deforestation.

Nor is that all. Inequalities of power and wealth also affect the two other fundamental determinants of market and quasi-market prices in the neoclassi-

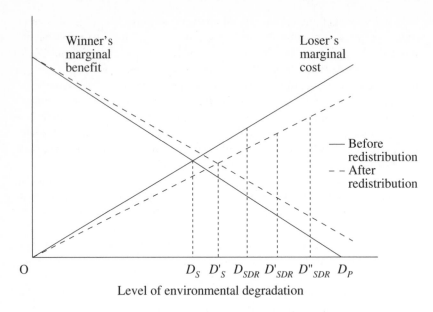

Figure 4.2   Effects of income redistribution on the level of environmental degradation

cal model: preferences and technology. Again, greater inequality can be expected to increase environmental degradation.

First consider preferences. As Becker (1983: 392) observes: '"preferences" can be manipulated and created through the information and misinformation provided by interested pressure groups.' A person's preference for clean air depends, among other things, on access to information about air quality and about the health effects of air pollution (see, for example, Bergstrom *et al.*, 1990). It also depends on how that person values air quality relative to other wants. Access to information and values both may be affected by the degree of inequality. With greater inequality, the relatively poor and powerless tend to have less access to information about environmental costs and, at the same time, to be more exposed to propaganda designed 'to make pollution seem palatable or worth the cost' (Galbraith 1973: 9). In terms of Figure 4.2, these preference effects cause a further downward shift in the marginal cost curve, and hence a further increase in the level of environmental degradation.

Similarly, if we shed the exogenous-technology assumption, and recognize that the pattern of technological change is subject to economic and political influences, this opens another route by which inequality may affect environmental valuations. The benefit that consumers derive from an environmentally degrading economic activity depends in part on the availability of less environmentally degrading alternatives. The latter may be limited by the power of vested interests to shape the path of technological change.

Let me illustrate by means of an example. A momentous technological choice in ground transportation is that between the internal combustion engine and the electric railway. Early in the twentieth century, the United States had an extensive electric rail system both within cities ('trolley cars') and between them. Today that network has been largely supplanted by motor vehicles plying concrete highways. The environmental costs of this historic social decision include vast air pollution and accelerated depletion of fossil fuels. In many cities – including Los Angeles, which today has the most unhealthful air quality in the nation – a consortium formed by General Motors, Standard Oil of California, and Firestone Tire Company played an important role in this transition: it purchased local rail lines, physically demolished them, sold the railroad rights-of-way, and converted mass transportation to buses. In 1949, the parties involved were convicted of conspiracy by a US Federal Court, and a symbolic fine of $1 was levied against the General Motors treasurer who masterminded the scheme. By this time, however, the nation's ground-transportation industry had been firmly reoriented to the new technological path.[8]

The marginal benefit of driving an automobile and spewing exhaust into the air is much enhanced if one lacks the option of travel by train. In terms of Figure 4.2, the effect is to raise the marginal benefit curve associated with this environmentally degrading activity, thereby increasing the level of environmental degradation. Of course, the triumph of the internal combustion engine in US ground transportation was not simply the result of conspiratorial machinations. But neither was it the result of perfect competition in the face of an exogenously demarcated production possibility frontier.

In sum, inequalities of wealth and power affect valuations of the costs and benefits of environmental degradation via the distribution of purchasing power, the shaping of preferences, and influences on the path of technological change. By each route, greater inequality tends to raise the valuation of benefits reaped by rich and powerful winners, relative to costs imposed on poor and less powerful losers.[9] These valuation effects reinforce the linkage between inequality and environmental degradation under the power-weighted social decision rule.

INEQUALITY AND ENVIRONMENTAL TIME PREFERENCE

One further dimension – time – can now be added to the analysis. Environmentally degrading activities often generate short-run benefits and long-run costs. The benefits from the indiscriminate logging of a forest, for example, accrue quickly with the sale of the timber, while costs in the form of soil erosion, disruption of hydrological cycles, and biodiversity loss can persist far into the future.

The rate of time preference refers to the willingness to trade present benefits (or costs) for future benefits (or costs). People with a higher rate of time preference place greater weight on the present. They are more willing to accept long-run costs for short-run benefits, and less willing to accept short-run costs for long-run gains. This notion can refer to financial savings as well as to environmental resources. It is possible, however, that the same people will apply different rates of time preference to different types of resources. My concern here is the rate applied to environmental resources, including clean air, clean water, soils and other 'natural capital.' I refer to this as the *rate of environmental time preference*.

How do inequalities of power and wealth affect concern for the long-term consequences of resource depletion or environmental pollution? I hypothesize that greater inequality leads to a higher rate of environmental time preference, that is, to less concern for the future, and that this is true for both rich and poor, though for different reasons.

First consider the impact of greater inequality, with average per capita income held constant, on the time preference of the poor. As poverty deepens, the imperatives of day-to-day survival compel the poor to degrade the environment. In Central America, for example, it drives poor peasants to cultivate steep hillsides, causing soil erosion. The linkage here runs from inequality to poverty to environmental degradation. If the poor are themselves the principal victims of this environmental degradation, the result is a 'vicious circle' in which, by trading short-run gains for long-run costs, the poor grow steadily poorer (Durning 1989; World Bank 1992).

In many instances, this undoubtedly is an important link between inequality and environmental degradation. But it is not the only link, nor necessarily the most important. In particular, it completely fails to account for environmental degradation by the rich. Yet, as I have suggested above, the latter may be more pervasive than environmental degradation by the poor.

How does greater inequality affect the rate of environmental time preference of the rich? The conventional assumption is that wealth and the rate of time preference are inversely related, not only among the poor, but throughout the entire range of wealth. Thus the richest individuals ostensibly have the highest savings rates – a key element in the proffered rationale for 'trickle-down' economic policies. If the same were true for the rate of environmental time preference, then greater inequality (and the resulting higher incomes for the rich, holding average income constant) would make the rich less myopic in their assessment of long-term environmental costs. Their lower rate of time preference would tend to offset the higher rate of the poor. Indeed, the net result of greater inequality conceivably could be a 'virtuous circle' in which the increased farsightedness of the rich raises long-run incomes not only for themselves but for society as a whole. This is simply an extension of the trickle-down logic to the environment. In my view, this would be too sanguine a conclusion. Indeed, it is plausible that increased inequality could have the opposite effect, *raising* the rate of environmental time preference of the rich.

Consider two hypothetical countries, both with large reserves of natural resources. In country A, a wealthy dictator monopolizes power and there is a high degree of economic inequality. Country B is identical in every respect, except that it has much higher degrees of political democracy (here defined as equity in the distribution of power) and economic equity. Which country will have the higher rate of environmental degradation?

The dictator of country A effectively controls its rate of resource extraction and the associated degree of environmental degradation. As a wealthy man, he may have a high financial savings rate and, in this respect, a low rate of time preference. But he may choose to hold the bulk of these savings outside his own country – in Swiss banks, Manhattan real estate, Mediterranean villas. Within his own country, meanwhile, the dictator's rate of *environmental* time preference may be quite high: he may choose to extract natural resources as quickly as possible, while shunning more costly methods which would mitigate the associated environmental impact. Is the disjuncture between the dictator's financial saving and his environmental dissaving a symptom of schizophrenia? Not if we recognize that the dictator's hold on political power – and with it, his *de facto* property rights over the country's natural resources – is inherently insecure. Eventually his oppressed fellow citizens may succeed in overthrowing him. The prudent dictator hedges against that possibility by feathering a foreign nest.

I submit that the dictator's degree of insecurity – and hence his rate of time preference with respect to the country's natural resources – is a function of the degree of political and economic inequality. The reason is simple: these inequalities undermine the ruler's legitimacy. For the moment, the dictator wields great power, but with time comes the possibility that power and wealth – perennial objects of contestation among individuals, groups, and classes – may be reallocated.

More generally, I advance the following hypothesis: The greater the degree of political and economic inequality, the higher the rate of environmental time preference of the rich. It is not only dictators who fear the reallocation of power and wealth. Inequalities may fatten foreign bank accounts, but they do not protect the environment at home.[10]

As a real-world example, consider the Philippines under President Ferdinand Marcos. During the two decades of Marcos's rule, the Philippines' rich tropical hardwood forests were rapidly felled for timber, with little effort to minimize the environmental impacts of deforestation. Exports of logs and lumber ranked among the country's top foreign-exchange earners until the early 1980s, when revenues collapsed due to the virtual depletion of economically accessible forests (for details, see Chapter 8). The cut-and-run philosophy of Marcos and his political associates was perfectly consistent with the foregoing analysis.

CONCLUSION

This chapter has advanced two central hypotheses. First, the extent of an environmentally degrading activity depends on the balance of power between the winners, who derive net benefits from the activity, and the losers, who bear net costs. When the winners are powerful relative to the losers, more environmental degradation occurs than in the reverse situation. This reflects the operation of what I term a power-weighted social decision rule.

Second, greater inequalities of power and wealth lead to more environmental degradation for three reasons: (a) the excess environmental degradation driven by powerful winners is not offset by the environmental degradation prevented by powerful losers; (b) inequality raises the valuation of benefits reaped by rich and powerful winners relative to costs imposed on poor and less powerful losers; and (c) inequality raises the rate of time preference applied to environmental resources by both the poor and the rich, by increasing their poverty and political insecurity, respectively.

Both hypotheses can be tested in empirical research. If accepted, they imply that democracy and equity are important not only as ends in themselves, but also as means to environmental protection.

NOTES

I am grateful to Katie Baird, Pranab Bardhan, Sam Bowles, Betsy Hartmann, Tad Homer-Dixon, Richard Wolff, and three referees for thoughtful comments on earlier drafts of this chapter. I also benefited from discussions by participants in the University of Massachusetts Political Economy Workshop, the Northeastern Universities Development Consortium Conference, and the Seminar on the Impact of Economic Policy on Sustainable Development in the Agricultural Sector held at the Inter-American Institute for Cooperation on Agriculture, Coronado, Costa Rica. The usual disclaimers apply.

1. I do not consider here the relative merits of the biocentric position that accords independent ethical value to the well-being of animals, plants, or ecosystems.
2. For interesting treatments of the first, see Martinez-Alier (1987: 156–71) and Norgaard and Howarth (1991).
3. I place 'efficient' in inverted commas because the valuations of benefits and costs by

which this term is defined vary with the distribution of endowments, preferences, and technology, as discussed below.

4. For an indictment of the environmental degradation under the Soviet power structure, see Komarov (1978). See also Pryde (1991) and Peterson (1993).

5. Environmental degradation per unit consumption is not necessarily constant across income classes. If degradation per unit were sufficiently greater for items with greater weight in the consumption basket of the poor, their demand could in theory account for more environmental degradation than that of the rich, notwithstanding their lower share of aggregate consumption. Empirically, it seems improbable that variations in degradation per unit consumption would yield this dramatic a result. Indeed, it is conceivable that degradation per unit consumption is *greater* for the rich; compare, for example, bicycles and automobiles.

6. For an exposition of consumers' and producers' surplus as measures of economic benefits, see Tietenberg (1992: 47–49).

7. The alternative method for valuation of health impacts of pollution, via the present value of forgone earnings, produces a similar result. See, for example, the memorandum of World Bank Chief Economist Lawrence Summers published in *The Economist* (1992).

8. For a brief account of this remarkable chapter of US history, see Commoner (1976:177–9). For details and debate, see Snell (1974), Whitt and Yago (1985), and Adler (1991).

9. By the same token, greater inequality would enhance the ability of rich and powerful losers to constrain environmentally degrading activities by poor and less powerful winners. As argued above, however, this offers, at most, meager solace.

10. Alternatively, we could say that inequality shifts the portfolio selection of the rich in favor of external as opposed to domestic assets. Since many domestic environmental resources are not fully private, they can be exchanged for external assets only if first harvested or mined. Resource depletion can here be interpreted in part as a social cost of privatization.

REFERENCES

Adler, S. (1991), 'The transformation of the Pacific Electric Railway,' *Urban Affairs Quarterly*, 27: 51–86.

Agarwal, B. (1992), 'The Gender and Environment Debate: Lessons from India,' *Feminist Studies*, 18(1): 119–58.

Becker, G.S. (1983), 'A theory of competition among pressure groups for political influence,' *Quarterly Journal of Economics*, 48(3): 371–400.

Bergstrom, J.C., Stoll, J.R. and Randall, A. (1990), 'The impact of information on environmental commodity valuation decisions,' *American Journal of Agricultural Economics*, 72 (3): 614–21.

Coase, R. (1960), 'The problem of social cost,' *Journal of Law and Economics*, 3: 1–44.

Commission on Racial Justice (1987), *Toxic Wastes and Race in the United States: A National Report on the Racial and Socio-economic Characteristics of Communities with Hazardous Waste Sites*, New York: United Church of Christ.

Commoner, B. (1976), *The Poverty of Power*, New York: Alfred A. Knopf.

Durning, A.B. (1989), 'Poverty and the environment: Reversing the downward spiral,' Worldwatch Paper no. 92, November, Washington, DC: Worldwatch Institute.

Economist, The (1992), 'Let them eat pollution,' 8 February: 66.

Ferguson, T. (1983), 'Party realignment and American industrial structure: The investment theory of political parties in historical perspective,' *Research in Political Economy*, 6: 1–82.

Galbraith, J.K. (1973), 'Power and the useful economist,' *American Economic Review*, 63 (1): 1–11.

Komarov, B. (1978), *The Destruction of Nature in the Soviet Union*, London: Pluto Press.

Martinez-Alier, J. (1987), *Ecological Economics: Energy, Environment and Society*, Oxford: Basil Blackwell.

Mendes, C. (1989), *Fight for the Forest: Chico Mendes in his Own Words*, London: Latin America Bureau.

Norgaard, R.B. and Howarth, R.B. (1991), 'Sustainability and discounting the future,' in R. Costanza (ed), *Ecological Economics: The Science and Management of Sustainability*, New York: Columbia University Press, pp. 88–101.

Olson, M. (1965), *The Logic of Collective Action*, Cambridge, MA: Harvard University Press.

Peterson, D.J. (1993), *Troubled Lands: The Legacy of Soviet Environmental Destruction*, Boulder, CO: Westview Press.

Pryde, P.R. (1991), *Environmental Management in the Soviet Union*, Cambridge and New York: Cambridge University Press.

Snell, B.C. (1974), *American Ground Transportation*, printed for the Subcommittee on Antitrust and Monopoly of the Committee on the Judiciary, US Senate, Washington, DC: US Government Printing Office.

Tietenberg, T. (1992), *Environmental and Natural Resource Economics*, 3rd edn., New York: HarperCollins.

United Nations Development Programme (1992), *Human Development Report 1992*, New York: Oxford University Press.

Whitt, J.A. and Yago, G. (1985), 'Corporate strategies and the decline of transit in US cities,' *Urban Affairs Quarterly*, 21: 37–65.

World Bank (1992), *World Development Report 1992*, New York: Oxford University Press.

5. Rethinking the environmental Kuznets curve

(with Mariano Torras)

INTRODUCTION

Mounting public concern over environmental issues has sparked efforts to understand more clearly the reasons for variations in the extent of environmental degradation. One way to address this question is through international comparisons, in which the dependent variable is some measure of environmental quality, and an array of variables that theory suggests might affect this measure – directly or otherwise – is included on the right-hand side of the regression equation. The studies (for example, Selden and Song 1994; Shafik 1994; Grossman and Krueger 1995) that have attempted this have used per capita income as the chief explanatory variable of interest.

The relationship between per capita income and environmental quality depends on scale, composition, and technology effects.[1] If the pollution intensity of aggregate output were fairly constant across countries, we would expect environmental quality to worsen with income, as greater output generates more pollution (the scale effect). On the other hand, environmental quality could improve with income if this scale effect were eclipsed by the combination of the two other effects. With increasing per capita income, the composition of output shifts among sectors that differ in their pollution intensity of output. For instance, the service sector may grow relative to the manufacturing sector. This composition effect can alter the pollution intensity of output. Furthermore, the various sectors of the economy may adopt less-polluting technologies, either because of market-driven technological advance (spurred in part by the internal benefits of resource conservation) or government regulation (including standards, taxes, and the creation of tradable emissions permits). There is no *a priori* reason to assume the relationship between income and environmental quality to be strictly monotonic. Instead, environmental quality may worsen with income within some ranges of income, but improve over others. Also, we should not necessarily expect the same relationship to hold for all dimensions of environmental quality. It is plausible, for example, that government regulatory responses are stronger when the effects of pollution lie primarily within national borders than when their impact is primarily transnational or global (Arrow *et al.* 1995; Max-Neef 1995).

Grossman and Krueger (1995), among others, find that for a number of environmental variables the relationship between per capita income and environmental degradation takes an inverted U-shaped form – that is, environmental quality initially worsens but ultimately improves with income. This apparent empirical relationship has been dubbed the 'environmental Kuznets curve,' because of its similarity to the relationship between per capita income and income inequality first suggested by Simon Kuznets (1955). Grossman and Krueger (1995) find evidence for such a relationship for 12 of the 14 air and water quality variables in their study.

Regrettably, the same incautious policy inference that was often drawn from the original Kuznets curve can be derived from the so-called environmental Kuznets curve. That is, if rising per capita income will ultimately induce countries to clean up their environments, then economic growth itself can be regarded as a remedy to environmental problems. As distributional concerns were subordinated to growth by proponents of 'trickle-down' economic development, so environmental concerns may be downplayed as a transitional phenomenon that growth will resolve in due course.[2]

Grossman and Krueger, like Kuznets before them, caution against such a reading of their findings. 'Even for those dimensions of environmental quality where growth seems to have been associated with improving conditions,' they write, 'there is no reason to believe the process is an automatic one … there is nothing at all inevitable about the relationships that have been observed in the past' (1995: 371–2). They suggest that 'an induced policy response' in the form of more stringent and more strictly enforced environmental standards, driven by citizen demand, has provided the strongest link between income and pollution. In so doing, they echo Kuznets's (1955: 28) original conclusion with respect to income distribution: 'Effective work in this field necessarily calls for a shift from market economics to political and social economy.'

This insight provides the starting point for this chapter. In particular, we investigate possible causal linkages between changes in income distribution, studied by Kuznets and many subsequent authors, and changes in pollution levels – a connection hitherto remarkably absent from discussions of the 'environmental Kuznets curve.' We hypothesize that changes in the distribution of power are central to the connections between the two phenomena.

The second section of this chapter briefly recaps the theory behind environmental Kuznets curves, summarizes our approach, and presents a model based upon it. The third section reviews the data and methodology utilized in our empirical analysis, and the results are then presented. The penultimate section examines the peaks and troughs in the relation between income and pollution, and their implications for the relationship between income growth and environmental quality. The final section summarizes our findings and offers some concluding remarks.

THE POLITICAL ECONOMY OF ENVIRONMENTAL KUZNETS CURVES

The environmental Kuznets curve is a 'reduced-form' relationship, in which the level of pollution is modeled as a function of per capita income without specifying the links between the two. Grossman and Krueger (1995: 359) characterize these missing links as 'environmental regulations, technology and industrial composition.' The reduced-form approach eliminates the need for data on these intervening structural variables, instead providing a direct estimate of the net effect of per capita income on pollution.

Two features of Grossman and Krueger's underlying structural model deserve mention. First, the industrial-composition effect that accompanies rising per capita income – whereby the share in total output of more pollution-intensive sectors, such as mining and manufacturing, declines, while the share of less pollution-intensive sectors, such as services, rises – may lower the marginal pollution intensity of output, but this cannot fully offset the scale effect (that is, the environmental impact resulting from the level of aggregate output) unless the more pollution-intensive sectors shrink absolutely. This could happen only if these sectors produce inferior goods, whose consumption falls with rising income, or if their products were replaced by imports. In general, the former condition seems unlikely to hold. The latter simply relocates pollution to other countries.

Second, following on this point, if total pollution declines with rising income, technological change is likely to play a key role. Hicks (1932) distinguished between 'autonomous' and 'induced' innovation: the former is exogenous, the latter endogenous to economic forces. If the technology effect is strong enough to cause total pollution to decline systematically across countries as per capita income rises, induced innovation is the likely cause. Market signals can contribute to the inducement process; for example, rising resource costs may encourage resource-conserving technological change, and a 'greening' of consumer demand may prompt firms to adopt cleaner technologies. But we suspect that government policies, including regulatory standards, pollution taxes, and the creation of tradable emission permits, have been the most important spur to pollution-reducing technological change.

Grossman and Krueger (1995: 372) likewise speculate that 'the strongest link between income and pollution in fact is via an induced policy response,' and that these policies in turn are induced by popular demand:

> As nations or regions experience greater prosperity, their citizens demand that more attention be paid to the noneconomic aspects of their living conditions. The richer countries, which tend to have relatively cleaner urban air and relatively cleaner river basins, also have relatively more stringent environmental standards and stricter enforcement of their environmental laws than the middle-income and poorer countries.

The public-good character of environmental quality means that effective demand requires solutions to market failure. Implicit in such policy-based explanations of the environmental Kuznets curve, then, is a simple theory of induced innovation: as per capita income rises, societies become better able to redress market failure. If this is empirically true, we can ask what characteristics of higher-income societies facilitate solutions to market failures. Is it per capita income *per se*, or other variables historically associated with it? Grossman and Krueger (1996: 120) hint at an answer:

> If environmental improvements are mediated by changes in government policy, then growth and development cannot be a substitute for environmental policy. In the absence of vigilance and advocacy in each and every location, there is always the possibility that greater output will mean greater consumption of (or waste of) scarce resources.

Why might 'vigilance and advocacy' (hereafter 'vigilance' for short) in a society increase with per capita income? One possibility is that individual demand for environmental quality rises. Another is that individuals gain greater power to make that demand effective through the political process.

Not everyone favors policies to reduce all sorts of pollution. Some individuals benefit from economic activities that generate pollution: otherwise these activities would not occur. The beneficiaries are producers who receive a 'pollution subsidy' (Templet 1995: 143) consisting of unspent pollution control dollars, and consumers who reap part of this subsidy via lower prices. In welfare-analytic terms, these benefits take the forms of producers' surplus and consumers' surplus, respectively. Other individuals adversely affected by pollution bear net costs. While the latter exercise vigilance in an attempt to establish or strengthen environmental controls, the beneficiaries exercise counter-vigilance in an attempt to prevent or weaken them.

Define b_i as the net benefit (net cost if $b_i < 0$) to the ith individual from a pollution-generating activity. The normative rule prescribed by benefit-cost analysis is to set the level of pollution so as to maximize aggregate net benefits, that is:

$$\max \sum_i b_i$$

Given declining marginal benefits from the pollution-generating activity and rising marginal costs from pollution, the socially efficient level of the activity is given by the familiar condition equating marginal benefit to marginal cost.

Chapter 4 describes actual environmental policy outcomes by means of a positive 'power-weighted social decision rule' (PWSDR) that maximizes net benefits weighted by power of those to whom they accrue:

$$\max \sum_i \pi_i b_i$$

where π_i = the power of the ith individual. Becker (1983) ascribes a comparable role to 'influence' in the determination of fiscal policy.

The PWSDR corresponds to the benefit-cost norm only in the special case where all individuals have equal power. When those who benefit from pollution-generating activities are more powerful than those who bear the costs, the PWSDR predicts inefficiently high levels of pollution. The opposite can occur too: if those who bear the costs of pollution are more powerful than those who derive the benefits, the PWSDR predicts inefficiently low levels of pollution.

Which situation is more prevalent depends on the relationship between b_i and π_i. If these are positively correlated, such that those who benefit from pollution-generating activities tend to be more powerful than those who bear the costs, then greater power inequality will be associated with more pollution.

There are good reasons to expect that net benefit from pollution-generating activities (b_i) is positively associated with individual income. Individuals with higher incomes generally own more assets and consume more commodities than those with lower incomes. Hence they can be expected to enjoy more producers' and consumers' surplus, including that created in pollution-generating activities. This is not to say that higher-income individuals want to breathe dirty air or to drink polluted water. But the vigilance with which they pursue these by public action is muted, if not overwhelmed, by the other arguments in their utility functions. The tension between their taste for environmental quality, on the one hand, and for consumer goods and profits, on the other, can be eased by channeling their demand for environmental quality into such private and semi-private goods as luxury housing, country clubs, and vacations in relatively pollution-free places.[3]

An individual's power (π_i), too, is likely to be correlated with his or her income. While this may seem evident to most people, remarkably few modern economists have seen fit to mention it. Simon Kuznets was among the exceptions. In 1963 he suggested that power inequality is a function of both income inequality and per capita income: 'One may argue that not only the welfare equivalents but also the power equivalents of the same relative income spread show a much wider range when the underlying average income is low than when it is high' (Kuznets 1963: 49). We will refer to this as Kuznets's 'unsung hypothesis,' since it has received far less attention than his earlier hypothesis of an inverted U-shaped relation between income inequality and per capita income.

Other variables, apart from income distribution, may also affect the distribution of power. These include individual attributes such as race, ethnicity, and gender, and the political framework through which these attributes and income are mapped to power. Adding these to Kuznets's unsung hypothesis, we get:

$$\Pi = \Pi(G, Y, X), \Pi_G < 0, \Pi_Y > 0 \qquad (5.1)$$

where Π = power distribution (with a higher value denoting a more equal distribution), G = income inequality, Y = per capita income, and the vector X consists of non-income determinants of power distribution.

The foregoing reasoning leads us to predict that greater power inequality will be associated with higher levels of pollution, as those who benefit from pollution-generating activities are better able to prevail against those who bear the costs. In this chapter we test this hypothesis. Our underlying structural model is:

$$POL = f(Y, \Pi, Z) \qquad (5.2)$$

where POL = the level of pollution, and Z is a vector of non-economic determinants of pollution levels. Per capita income (Y) is included to allow for possible effects on pollution aside from those mediated by power inequality. In the absence of direct measures of power distribution, we use variables drawn from the right-hand side of (5.1) as proxies for Π.

We will test the empirical validity of these propositions by means of the following model:

$$POL = \alpha + \beta_1 Y + \beta_2 Y^2 + \beta_3 Y^3 + \delta_1 GINI + \delta_2 LIT \\ + \delta_3 RIGHTS + \gamma_i Z_i + \mu, \qquad (5.3)$$

where POL = the pollution variable being tested; Y = per capita income; $GINI$ = the Gini coefficient of income inequality; LIT = the literacy rate; $RIGHTS$ = political rights and civil liberties; and Z_i is a vector of other (primarily geographical) covariates, such as dummy variables for central cities and coastal zones, which are used in the subnational-level regressions, and urbanization, which is used in the national-level regressions.

All equations are estimated by ordinary least squares (OLS).[4] For five of our pollution variables we have data from the same sites for several years, but it is not possible to use a fixed-effects model to control for omitted country-specific variables since the power inequality variables (*GINI*, *LIT*, and *RIGHTS*) have unique values for each country. An attempt to control for fixed effects would hence result in perfect linear dependence. This problem could be mitigated by compiling time-series data for the power inequality variables, but this is beyond the scope of the present study. Furthermore, any fixed-effects estimation focuses on time-series changes, whereas cross-country variations are of primary interest in this analysis.[5]

DATA

Dependent Variables

Altogether we test seven distinct pollution variables. Three atmospheric pollution variables and two water pollution variables are taken from the Global Environment Monitoring System (GEMS) data set, which includes observations from various locations around the world. The other two variables are national-level data on the percentage of the population with access to safe water and sanitation facilities, aspects of environmental quality of particular relevance to the well-being of the poor in low-income countries. A complete variable list is provided in Table 5.A1.

The GEMS Data Set

The three atmospheric pollution variables (sulfur dioxide, smoke, and heavy particles) and two water variables (dissolved oxygen and fecal coliform) from the GEMS data set were also investigated by Grossman and Krueger. We employ the same data, covering the years from 1977 to 1991. The GEMS air pollution data contain observations from 18 to 52 cities in 19 to 42 countries (varying depending on the pollutant). The GEMS water pollution data contain observations from up to 287 stations in 58 countries. All these data are location-specific; the GEMS data set contains no aggregate national measures of pollution. In all cases except for dissolved oxygen, higher values indicate inferior environmental quality; in the case of dissolved oxygen the reverse is true.

Each of the dependent variables we test represents some concentration level, with the exception of the variable for fecal coliform. As done by Grossman and Krueger (1995), $\log(1 + \mu)$ is used as a measure of fecal coliform concentration, where μ is the concentration level. The reasons are threefold: (a) the coliform grow exponentially; (b) the distribution is positively skewed; and (c) we cannot simply use $\log(\mu)$ because many zero readings exist (where coliform is below the minimum detectable level) and one cannot take the log of zero.

National-level Pollution Variables

Our national-level variables are the percentage of the population with access to safe water and the percentage with access to sanitation. These data are taken from the United Nations Development Programme (1994) and contain no time-series dimension, unlike the GEMS data.

Explanatory Variables

Income
Per capita income is measured in real purchasing power parity (PPP) adjusted dollars. Like Grossman and Krueger (1995) and Shafik (1994), we use a cubic functional form for the per capita income variable. An attraction of the cubic form is that while it permits a simple quadratic (U-shaped) relationship (when the estimated coefficient on the cubic term is approximately zero), it allows for a second turning point (when it is non-zero). In the case of the GEMS data set, we use the same income data as Grossman and Krueger, taken from Summers and Heston (1991). In the case of the national-level variables, we use 1991 income from the United Nations Development Programme (1994).

Income inequality
As a measure of income inequality we use Gini ratios reported by the World Bank (1996).[6] Three limitations of the available data should be noted. First, there remain many countries for which income distribution data are not available. Hence, using this variable diminishes our sample size. Second, despite recent efforts at the World Bank to standardize the data, methodological inconsistencies remain. For example, for some countries the Gini ratios refer to expenditure rather than income. Finally, the accuracy of some of these data is open to doubt. We find it surprising, for example, that the Gini ratio reported for Peru is lower than that reported for Costa Rica, a country with a history of social democracy that is rare among Latin American nations.

Literacy
As another proxy for power equality, we use adult literacy rates for males and females in the year 1992, as reported by the United Nations Development Programme (1994). To the extent that literacy brings greater access to infor-

mation, and access to information is correlated with power, countries with higher literacy rates can be said to enjoy a more equitable distribution of power.

Political rights and civil liberties

As a further measure of power equality, we employ an aggregate of two variables reported in Finn (1996): political rights and civil liberties in the year 1995. Each is measured on a one-to-seven scale, with one meaning the most freedom, and seven the least. We add the two, and subtract this sum from 14 to obtain a 0–12 scale, with higher values representing greater freedom.

Urbanization

We include the urbanization rate as an explanatory variable in our national-level regressions. This is the percentage of the country's population living in urban areas, as reported by the United Nations Development Programme (1994). Though urbanization is often associated with greater levels of pollution, it may also facilitate some environmental improvements, for example through economies of scale in the provision of sanitation facilities.

GEMS control variables

The control variables included in the GEMS air pollution data set are the monitoring station's proximity to a coastline, the type of area (industrial, residential, commercial) in which the station is located, the city's population density, and the year in which the measurement was taken. The control variables for the water pollution data set are mean water temperature and the year in which the measurement was taken.[7]

RESULTS

We have estimated equation (5.3) for each of the pollution variables described in the previous section. For comparative purposes, we first estimated the equation with only income and the geographical control variables on the right-hand side. We then included the three power inequality variables – the Gini ratio of income distribution, literacy, and political and civil rights – as additional regressors.

Table 5.1 presents our regression results, excluding the inequality variables, for the five pollution variables drawn from the GEMS data set. These results are similar to those of Grossman and Krueger (1995).[8] In the cases of sulfur dioxide and smoke, we obtain the 'Kuznetsian' inverted-U relation: pollution initially rises with per capita income and then declines. However,

Table 5.1   *The determinants of pollution (GEMS variables): excluding inequality*

Explanatory variable	Sulfur dioxide	Smoke	Heavy particles	Dissolved oxygen	Fecal coliform
Income	$9.71E^{-3**}$	$2.69E^{-2**}$	$-6.38E^{-2**}$	$2.55E^{-4*}$	$3.94E^{-4**}$
	(4.22)	(2.51)	(−7.29)	(2.01)	(2.46)
Income squared	$-1.60E^{-6**}$	$-4.37E^{-6**}$	$4.67E^{-6**}$	$-3.84E^{-8*}$	$-2.23E^{-8}$
	(−5.10)	(−2.51)	(4.01)	(−2.06)	(−0.94)
Income cubed	$6.06E^{-11**}$	$1.96E^{-10*}$	$-1.17E^{-10**}$	$1.99E^{-12**}$	$-3.58E^{-13}$
	(5.07)	(2.24)	(−2.75)	(2.63)	(−0.37)
Central city	13.42^{**}	11.86^{**}	15.44^{*}	—	—
	(6.01)	(2.74)	(2.13)		
Coast	-6.77^{**}	-21.15^{**}	-51.33^{**}	—	—
	(−3.43)	(−5.63)	(−8.57)		
Industrial	3.66	1.91	30.96^{**}	—	—
	(1.38)	(0.40)	(3.56)		
Residential	−2.11	−5.18	7.15	—	—
	(−0.82)	(−1.18)	(0.84)		
Population density	$-1.46E^{-6}$	$1.43E^{-4***}$	$-1.38E^{-4*}$	—	—
	(−0.07)	(4.59)	(−1.70)		
Year	-1.65^{**}	−0.77	0.50	-0.06^{*}	0.02
	(−5.48)	(−1.45)	(0.50)	(−2.21)	(0.46)
Mean water temperature	—	—	—	-0.16^{**}	0.09^{**}
				(−11.22)	(4.68)
Adjusted R^2	0.15	0.27	0.61	0.21	0.06
N	1188	405	854	1931	1484

Notes:
t-ratios in parentheses.
*   Statistically significant at 5% level.
**   Statistically significant at 1% level.

the statistically significant positive coefficients on the cubic term imply that these pollutants eventually resume a rising trend (a point to which we return in the next section). Sulfur dioxide pollution also shows a secular trend to diminish over time (indicated by the statistically significant negative coefficient on the year). Airborne heavy particles monotonically diminish with income (a plot of the curve shows a flattening in the middle-income range due to the positive coefficient on income squared). As expected, central city locations are associated with higher levels of these air pollutants, and coastal locations with lower levels.

Dissolved oxygen in water improves with income (recall that more dissolved oxygen indicates better water quality). Fecal coliform pollution displays an inverted-U pattern, first rising with income and then declining, though the

*Table 5.2   The determinants of pollution (national-level variables):
excluding inequality*

Explanatory variable	Safe water (%)	Sanitation (%)
Income	$8.98E^{-3**}$	$1.74E^{-2**}$
	(3.46)	(5.42)
Income squared	$-6.99E^{-7**}$	$-1.31E^{-6**}$
	(−2.48)	(−3.76)
Income cubed	$1.79E^{-11*}$	$3.14E^{-11**}$
	(1.90)	(2.69)
Urbanization rate	0.31^{**}	0.17
	(2.78)	(1.25)
Adjusted R^2	0.64	0.69
N	82	79

Notes:
t-ratios in parentheses.
*   Statistically significant at 5% level.
**   Statistically significant at 1% level.

quadratic and cubic terms here are not statistically significant. Higher water temperatures are associated, as expected, with poorer water quality.

Table 5.2 presents the comparable results for the two national-level environmental quality variables. The percentages of the population with access to safe water and sanitation initially rise with income, then dip slightly, and then resume rising.[9] Urbanization is associated with better access to safe water and sanitation (though not statistically significant for the latter), indicating that in this important respect it tends to have a positive effect on environmental quality.

In testing the impact of the inequality variables, we allow for the possibility that their effects may differ in low-income and high-income countries, as suggested by Kuznets in his unsung hypothesis. Using a $5000 per capita income (in PPP-adjusted dollars) as a dividing line, we create dummy variables for low- and high-income countries. By interacting these with the inequality variables, we estimate separate coefficients for the latter for the two sets of countries.

Our results are reported in Table 5.3.[10] Comparing these with the results in Tables 5.1 and 5.2, we find that the statistical significance of the income effects generally diminishes when the inequality variables are included as regressors. The most striking cases are those of smoke and heavy particles, where the income effects recede into statistical insignificance.

Table 5.3 The determinants of pollution: including inequality

Explanatory variable	Sulfur dioxide	Smoke	Heavy particles	Dissolved oxygen	Fecal coliform	Safe water (%)	Sanitation (%)
Income	0.01^{**}	0.01	0.02	-8.00E^{-5**}	3.89E^{-4}	0.01^{**}	0.02^{**}
	(3.28)	(0.46)	(1.27)	(-3.16)	(1.12)	(4.06)	(4.02)
Income squared	-1.81E^{-6**}	-2.52E^{-6}	-1.76E^{-7}	9.88E^{-8**}	-4.15E^{-8}	-9.72E^{-7**}	-1.07E^{-6**}
	(-3.91)	(-0.79)	(-0.11)	(3.17)	(-0.99)	(-3.08)	(-2.81)
Income cubed	6.42E^{-11**}	1.21E^{-10}	-2.37E^{-11}	-2.64E^{-12*}	8.99E^{-13}	2.39E^{-11*}	2.35E^{-11}
	(3.87)	(0.83)	(-0.44)	(-2.26)	(0.57)	(2.32)	(1.89)
Gini ratio (low-income)	114.20^{**}	106.66^{**}	-508.10^{**}	6.17^{**}	-1.52	-48.00^{**}	-10.84
	(5.69)	(2.92)	(-5.80)	(4.84)	(-0.83)	(-2.58)	(-0.47)
Gini ratio (high-income)	-87.07^{**}	-40.09	96.35	-2.89	-6.64^{**}	-30.51	-23.96
	(-3.51)	(-0.90)	(1.28)	(-1.33)	(-2.37)	(-0.96)	(-0.63)
Literacy rate (low-income)	-0.72^{**}	-0.46	-4.61^{**}	0.02^{*}	0.01	-0.12	0.38^{**}
	(-4.13)	(-0.99)	(-10.42)	(2.25)	(1.24)	(-1.07)	(2.81)
Literacy rate (high-income)	-0.38	2.20^{**}	-10.42^{**}	0.11^{**}	0.07^{**}	-0.41	0.13
	(-1.13)	(3.00)	(-9.07)	(4.67)	(2.42)	(-1.29)	(0.35)
Rights (low-income)	-5.24^{**}	-6.18^{**}	-16.67^{**}	0.08^{*}	-0.19^{**}	2.33E^{-3}	-0.34
	(-8.36)	(-4.48)	(-10.50)	(2.02)	(-3.43)	(0.00)	(-0.45)
Rights (high-income)	1.42	-18.59^{**}	2.88	-0.51^{**}	-0.48^{**}	1.18	1.73
	(0.92)	(-4.28)	(0.63)	(-4.13)	(-3.13)	(0.69)	(0.84)
Adjusted R^2	0.22	0.35	0.74	0.23	0.08	0.66	0.72
N	1188	405	854	1931	1484	82	79

Notes:
t-ratios in parentheses.
* Statistically significant at 5% level.
** Statistically significant at 1% level.

Income inequality, measured by the Gini ratio, has mixed effects. In the cases of sulfur dioxide and smoke, greater income inequality is associated with more pollution in the low-income countries, but not in the high-income countries. Similarly, in low-income countries income inequality negatively affects the percentage of the population with access to safe water. These findings are consistent with our hypothesis as to the relation between inequality and pollution, and with Kuznets's unsung hypothesis. In the cases of heavy particles and dissolved oxygen, however, we obtain contrary results: greater income inequality in the low-income countries appears to be associated with less pollution. Given the questionable quality of the income-distribution data, however, we do not place great confidence in these findings.

The impact of literacy is generally consistent with our hypothesis. In the low-income countries, literacy is statistically significantly associated with better environmental quality (less pollution) in the cases of sulfur dioxide, heavy particles, dissolved oxygen, and sanitation; in the high-income countries, too, it has statistically significant favorable effects on heavy particles, dissolved oxygen, and fecal coliform pollution. Only in the case of smoke in the high-income countries do we obtain a statistically significant coefficient on literacy with the 'wrong' sign.

The estimated coefficients on political rights and civil liberties lend further support to our hypothesis. In the low-income countries, a higher rights score is associated with statistically significant improvements in levels of sulfur dioxide, smoke, heavy particles, dissolved oxygen, and fecal coliform; in no case do we find statistically significant contrary effects. In the high-income countries, the impact of the rights variable tends to be weaker: we find statistically significant favorable effects on smoke and fecal coliform, but a statistically significant opposite effect on dissolved oxygen.

For each of our seven pollution indicators, one or more of the power inequality variables thus turns out to have a statistically significant effect in the predicted direction. Their inclusion in the regressions generally reduces the statistical significance of per capita income as a determinant of environmental quality. Literacy and rights show stronger and more consistent effects than the Gini ratio, suggesting that these are better proxies for power inequality.[11] The inequality effects tend to be strongest in the low-income countries, suggesting that Kuznets's insight – that the 'power equivalents' of a given income distribution show a wider range when average income is low – applies to the power equivalents of literacy and rights as well. In sum, our results provide fairly robust support for the hypothesis that greater inequality in the distribution of power leads to more pollution.

PEAKS AND TROUGHS: A CAUTIONARY NOTE ON HIGH-INCOME COUNTRIES

The results presented in the preceding section suggest that rising per capita income can be accompanied by improvements in air and water quality, and that improvements in the distribution of power play an important role in this outcome. Does this imply that we can be complacent about environmental problems in those countries that have successfully made the transition to high income and declining pollution levels? We think not. An interesting feature of the literature on the environmental Kuznets curve, which marks a departure from the original Kuznetsian literature on income distribution, is the common use of a cubic functional form for income. This allows for the possibility that a downturn in pollution (at the peak of the inverted U) can be followed by a later upturn; that is, a reversal of the tendency for pollution levels to decline with further increases in per capita income.

In many cases, this is precisely what we observe. Table 5.4 presents the relevant peaks and troughs calculated from our regression results. For example, the levels of sulfur dioxide and smoke peak at a per capita income in the neighborhood of $4000 (in PPP$). Grossman and Krueger (1995: 367) report similar results. If we consider per capita income values only up to $15,000, we see evidence of the 'Kuznets U,' but considering values of income greater

Table 5.4   Peaks and troughs of pollution functions

Variable	Specification	Peak	Trough
Sulfur dioxide	Excluding inequality	$3890	$15425
	Including inequality	$3360	$14034
Smoke	Excluding inequality	$4350	$10510
	Including inequality	Income not statistically significant	
Heavy particles	Excluding inequality	Monotonic decrease	
	Including inequality	Income not statistically significant	
Dissolved oxygen	Excluding inequality	Monotonic increase	
	Including inequality	$19865	$5085
Fecal coliform	Excluding inequality	Monotonic increase	
	Including inequality	Income not statistically significant	
Access to safe water	Excluding inequality	$11255	$14925
	Including inequality	$6900	$20215
Access to sanitation	Excluding inequality	$10957	$16852
	Including inequality	Monotonic increase	

than $15,000 yields a quite different story: beyond a trough around this income level, the levels of both pollutants rise with income. Grossman and Krueger do not comment on these subsequent upturns, which are apparent for eight of the twelve pollution variables for which they find support for the environmental Kuznets curve hypothesis. These upturns can hardly be called irrelevant; the income levels at which they occur are not terribly high – indeed, many industrialized countries have already exceeded them.

These findings imply that beyond some point high income levels, rather than being conducive to further improvement in air and water quality, can have the opposite effect. Whether this is true, and if so, why, are questions that deserve further study. One possibility is that the scale effect overshadows the composition and technology effects, as the scope for further improvements in the distribution of power is reduced, or as these improvements generate diminishing returns in terms of pollution-reducing technological change. Another possibility is that rising per capita income in the high-income countries has been associated with increasing power inequality. In either event, our results do not offer grounds for complacency regarding the environmental impacts of growth in the high-income countries.

CONCLUDING REMARKS

This study brings 'political and social economy,' in Kuznets's (1955) phrase, to bear on the analysis of the relationship between per capita income and pollution. We believe, like Grossman and Krueger (1995, 1996), that citizens' demand and 'vigilance and advocacy' are often critical in inducing policies and technological changes which reduce pollution. However, we do not regard these as simple functions of average income. For the reasons elaborated in the preceding chapter, we hypothesize that more equitable distributions of power tend, *ceteris paribus*, to result in better environmental quality.

Our regression results generally are consistent with this hypothesis. Literacy and rights appear to be particularly strong predictors of pollution levels in the low-income countries. The estimated effects of per capita income on pollution generally weaken once we account for inequality effects, but they do not disappear altogether. In those cases where higher per capita income continues to be associated with less pollution, there are at least three possible explanations. First, it is likely that our proxy variables do not fully capture income-related changes in power inequality; better controlling for these might further weaken the pure income effects. Second, individual demand for environmental quality may rise with income – and rise more strongly than demand for other goods and services, the production and consumption of which generate pollution – such that even with an unchanged distribution of power, there is greater politically effective demand for environmental quality.[12] Finally, as average income in a given country rises, pollution-intensive production may be relocated to lower-income countries. If so, this may reflect power inequalities among countries as well as within them.[13]

One policy implication of our findings is that the growth of per capita income in developing countries can be accompanied by improvements in at least some important dimensions of environmental quality. We agree with Grossman and Krueger (1996: 122) that 'putting brakes on economic growth in the developing world is not an acceptable, or even a wise, response to the pressing environmental concerns of our time.' To this, however, we would add two further policy implications.

First, promoting more equitable power distributions in the developing world is a wise response to environmental concerns. Our findings indicate that efforts to achieve a more equal distribution of power, via more equitable income distribution, wider literacy, and greater political rights and civil liberties, can positively affect environmental quality. The effects of these variables appear to be particularly strong in low-income countries. From an environmental standpoint, then, the distribution of power is not a peripheral concern.

Second, we cannot assume that environmental improvements will continue to accompany further growth of per capita income in those countries that have already attained high average incomes. For countries in the upper-income range, there is evidence that rising average income is associated with renewed deterioration in some dimensions of environmental quality. The extent to which this trade-off can be relaxed through social, political, and technological changes remains an open question.

APPENDIX

Table 5.A1   Variable list

Variable	Mean	N	Source
SO_2 median $(\mu g/m^3)$[a]	33.23	1297	GEMS
Smoke median $(\mu g/m^3)$	42.56	484	GEMS
Heavy particles median $(\mu g/m^3)$	149.68	916	GEMS
Dissolved O_2 mean (mg/l)[b]	7.9	2054	GEMS
Fecal coliform mean log$(1 + \mu g/100$ ml$)$	5.58	1569	GEMS
% access to safe water	72.38	142	United Nations Development Programme (1994)
% access to sanitation	65.24	139	United Nations Development Programme (1994)
Per capita income (dollars)	6859.25	—	Summers and Heston (1991);[c] United Nations Development Programme (1994)
Coast (1 = close to coast, 0 = not)	0.56	—	GEMS
Central city (1= central city, 0 = not)	0.54	—	GEMS
Industrial (1= industrial, 0 = not)	0.29	—	GEMS
Residential (1= residential, 0 = not)	0.36	—	GEMS
Population density (pop./sq.mile)	34970.5	—	GEMS
Year	—	—	GEMS
Mean water temperature (°C)[d]	19.58	—	GEMS
Gini coefficient	0.41	—	World Bank (1996)
% literate	75.4	—	United Nations Development Programme (1994)
Political rights and civil liberties (0 to 12 scale)	6.35	—	Finn (1996)
% urbanized	50.1	—	United Nations Development Programme (1994)

Notes:
a   Micrograms per cubic meter.
b   Milligrams per liter.
c   Includes extrapolations made by Grossman and Krueger for years after 1988.
d   For missing values temperature was estimated from latitude data.

NOTES

We wish to thank Robert Ayres, Katie Baird, Sam Bowles, Sander de Bruyn, Neha Khanna, Manfred Max-Neef, Bernie Morzuch, Dale Rothman, Cleve Willis, the participants in the technical session on the Environmental Kuznets Curve at the Fourth Biennial Meeting of the International Society for Ecological Economics, and participants in the Economic History and Economic Development Workshop at the University of Massachusetts, Amherst, for helpful comments on earlier versions of this chapter. We are especially grateful to Maggie Winslow, who first called our attention to the *Freedom House* data. Also, we thank Gene Grossman for directing us to the location on the internet (http://irs.princeton.edu) where the GEMS data can be found, and Eileen Atallah, Trina Hosmer, and Dee Weber for their assistance in data formatting.

1. For a more detailed explanation of these effects, see Grossman (1995) or Grossman and Krueger (1995).
2. This concern has been voiced by various critics. For example, Arrow *et al.* (1995) caution that economic growth is 'no substitute' for environmental policy. Ayres (1995) considers this an understatement, and dismisses as 'false and pernicious nonsense' the idea that economic growth is good for the environment. Kaufmann and Cleveland (1995) make the important related point that long-run sustainability depends not simply on the level of emissions (and resource depletion) but also on the capacity of natural systems to absorb and process wastes (and renew resources).
3. It is possible (though not certain) that within a given society, the marginal pollution intensity of consumption (including pollution generated in the production and transport of consumer goods and services, as well as in the act of consumption itself) declines with rising individual income. Even were this so, greater income inequality (that is, redistribution of income from poor to rich) could be associated with greater pollution, if the industrial-composition effect of this redistribution were outweighed by its adverse impact on power inequality and thereby on vigilance, regulation, and pollution-reducing technological change. This would be depicted graphically by an outward shift of the curve relating the marginal pollution intensity of consumption to individual income. Our expectation that income inequality is associated with higher levels of pollution is premised on the hypothesis that such technology effects do, in fact, outweigh any distribution-driven industrial composition effects.
4. Generalized least squares (GLS) yields, without exception, regression coefficients which are virtually identical to the OLS coefficients, but with much smaller standard errors and hence even higher statistical significance. More important, in our view, is the economic significance of the estimated coefficients (McCloskey and Ziliak 1996: 98).
5. Year-to-year variations in income inequality, literacy, or rights within a given country would be unlikely to have strong effects on the level of pollution. In any event, our interest is longer-term determinants of inter-country variations in pollution levels.
6. The Gini ratio is a standard measure of income inequality employed by economists. Hypothetically it ranges from 0 (perfect equality) to 1 (all income received by one individual). For details on its derivation, see Kakwani (1980). In the case of the OECD countries, we computed Gini ratios from the quintile data reported in the same source.
7. Following Grossman and Krueger, missing mean temperature observations are estimated from a regression of temperature on latitude for those observations (the majority) for which data are available.
8. In addition to current income, Grossman and Krueger include average income in the preceding three years as a lagged measure. We have not done so here, since lagged income is strongly collinear with current income. Grossman and Krueger themselves note (p. 361) that 'including just current (or just lagged) GDP per capita does not qualitatively change the results.' Our total numbers of observations differ slightly from those reported by Grossman and Krueger for reasons which are not clear.
9. Shafik (1994) reports similar results for access to safe water and urban sanitation.

10. For reasons of space we omit the coefficients on the geographical control variables from Table 5.3.
11. This could be because literacy and rights are intrinsically more important determinants of the distribution of power, or because the Gini data are unreliable, or both.
12. Note that politically effective demand for public goods requires institutional solutions to the free-rider problem.
13. As Arrow *et al.* (1995: 92) observe, 'reductions in one pollutant in one country may involve increases in other pollutants in the same country or transfers of pollutants to other countries.' In a study of industrial composition effects, Rock (1996) finds evidence that developing countries with more outward-oriented trade policies tend to have higher pollution intensities of GDP. Inequality across nations and its consequences for the global environment is an important area for future empirical work.

REFERENCES

Arrow, K., Bolin, B., Costanza, R., Dasgupta, P., Folke, C., Holling, C.S., Jansson, B.-O., Levin, S., Mäler, K.-G., Perrings, C. and Pimentel, D. (1995), 'Economic growth, carrying capacity, and the environment,' *Science*, 268: 520–1.

Ayres, R.U. (1995), 'Economic growth: politically necessary but *not* environmentally friendly,' *Ecological Economics*, 15: 97–9.

Becker, G. (1983), 'A theory of competition among pressure groups for political influence,' *Quarterly Journal of Economics*, 48: 371–400.

Finn, J. (ed.) (1996), *Freedom in the World: Political Rights and Civil Liberties*, New York: Freedom House.

Grossman, G.M. (1995), 'Pollution and growth: what do we know?' in I. Goldin and A. Winters (eds), *Sustainable Economic Development: Domestic and International Policy*, Cambridge: Cambridge University Press, pp. 19–50.

Grossman, G.M. and Krueger, A.B. (1995), 'Economic growth and the environment,' *Quarterly Journal of Economics*, 60: 353–77.

Grossman, G.M. and Krueger, A.B. (1996), 'The inverted-U: what does it mean?', *Environment and Development Economics*, 1: 119–22.

Hicks, J.R. (1932), *The Theory of Wages*, London: Macmillan.

Kakwani, N. (1980), *Income Inequality and Poverty: Methods of Estimation and Policy Applications*, New York and Oxford: Oxford University Press.

Kaufmann, R.K. and Cleveland, C.J. (1995), 'Measuring sustainability: needed – an interdisciplinary approach to an interdisciplinary concept,' *Ecological Economics*, 15: 109–12.

Kuznets, S. (1955), 'Economic growth and income inequality,' *American Economic Review*, 1: 1–28.

Kuznets, S. (1963), 'Quantitative aspects of the economic growth of nations,' *Economic Development and Cultural Change*, 11 (2/II): 1–80.

Max-Neef, M. (1995), 'Economic growth and quality of life: a threshold hypothesis,' *Ecological Economics*, 15: 115–18.

McCloskey, D.N. and Ziliak, S.T. (1996), 'The standard error of regressions,' *Journal of Economic Literature*, 34: 97-114.

Rock, M.T. (1996), 'Pollution intensity of GDP and trade policy: can the World Bank be wrong?', *World Development*, 24(3): 471–9.

Selden, T. and Song, D. (1994), 'Environmental quality and development: is there a Kuznets curve for air pollution emissions?', *Journal of Environmental Economics and Management*, 27: 147–62.

Shafik, N. (1994), 'Economic development and environmental quality: an econometric analysis,' *Oxford Economic Papers*, 46: 757–73.

Summers, R. and Heston, A. (1991), 'The Penn World Table (Mark 5): an expanded
set of international comparisons, 1950–1988,' *Quarterly Journal of Economics*, 56:
327–68.

Templet, P.H. (1995), 'Grazing the commons: an empirical analysis of externalities,
subsidies and sustainability,' Ecological Economics, 12: 141–59.

United Nations Development Programme (1994), *Human Development Report 1994*,
New York and Oxford: Oxford University Press.

World Bank (1996), *World Development Report 1996*, New York and Oxford: Oxford
University Press.

6. Power distribution, the environment, and public health

(with Andrew R. Klemer, Paul H. Templet, and Cleve E. Willis)

INTRODUCTION

Environmentally degrading economic activities generate both winners and losers. The winners derive net benefits in the form of producers' and consumers' surplus; the losers bear net costs arising from environmental externalities. Starting with this premise, Chapter 4 advanced two hypotheses: first, social choices governing environmental degradation systematically favor more powerful agents over less powerful agents; and second, wider inequalities of power tend to result in greater environmental degradation.

The first hypothesis, on the identities of winners and losers, generates the prediction that the distribution of environmental costs will be correlated with other power-related variables such as income, race, and ethnicity. In recent years a substantial literature on such correlations has emerged in the USA. Case studies have drawn attention to links between socioeconomic status and pollution exposure in various locations, from Chester, Pennsylvania and Louisiana's 'Cancer Alley' to South Central and East Los Angeles.[1] Pioneering statistical studies by Bullard (1983) and the US General Accounting Office (1983) found correlations between the siting of waste dumps and the racial composition of surrounding communities.[2] Recent studies by Perlin et al. (1995) and Brooks and Sethi (1997) similarly found emissions of airborne toxic pollutants to be correlated with race and ethnicity at the county and postal zip-code levels. In response to concerns that minority and low-income populations bear a disproportionately high share of environmental costs, President Clinton's Executive Order 12898 of February 1994 established an Interagency Working Group on Environmental Justice. How did this help?

This chapter, like Chapter 5, presents a test of the second hypothesis, on the extent of environmental costs as opposed to their incidence. This hypothesis suggests that with greater inequality in the distribution of power, those agents with more power are able to impose high external costs on those with less

67

power, and that this effect is not fully offset by the diminished ability of the less powerful to impose external costs on the more powerful. If this is so, power inequalities affect the size of the pollution pie, as well as how it is sliced.

In this chapter we test this hypothesis using cross-sectional data for the 50 US states.[3] The choice of the state as the unit of analysis is motivated by two considerations. First, state governments play an important role in the formulation and enforcement of environmental policies, and the importance of state policies is increasing as the Federal government devolves greater responsibilities to them. Second, the possible confounding effects of population movements in response to environmental conditions – for example, the migration of low-income groups to environmentally degraded locales in response to falling property values – are likely to be weaker at the state level than at more disaggregated levels such as the county or postal zip-code area (Been 1994).

The remainder of the chapter is organized as follows. We first present a model linking the distribution of power to environmental policy, environmental stress, and public health. We then derive a measure of interstate variations in the distribution of power, discuss the other data used in our analysis, and present the econometric results. Finally, we offer some concluding observations on the policy implications of our findings.

THE POLITICAL ECONOMY OF ENVIRONMENTAL COSTS: A RECURSIVE MODEL

This section presents a recursive model running from power distribution to environmental policy to environmental stress to public health outcomes. Each of these links is examined in turn.

Power Distribution and its Determinants

Power is difficult to measure. We can construct indirect measures, however, based on power-related variables. In this study we use four variables for this purpose: voter participation, tax fairness, Medicaid accessibility, and educational attainment. Higher voter participation is taken to indicate a more equal distribution of power.[4] Tax fairness and Medicaid accessibility are taken to reflect the influence of power distribution on the revenue and expenditure sides of state fiscal policies, respectively. A higher level of educational attainment is taken to indicate a more equal distribution of power, on the assumption that there are important links between information and power.[5] In the next section, we derive a measure of interstate variations in the distribution of power by means of a principal components analysis of these four variables.

An analysis of determinants of variations in this measure can shed light on its validity and on the origins of power disparities. Following Chapters 4 and 5, we hypothesize that power distribution (Π) is a function of income inequality (G), the level of per capita income (Y), and a vector of non-income determinants (X):

$$\Pi = \Pi(G, Y, X), \Pi_G < 0, \Pi_Y > 0 \qquad (6.1)$$

where a higher value of Π denotes a more equal distribution of power. Greater income inequality is expected to lead, *ceteris paribus*, to greater power inequality.[6] Building on Kuznets's (1963: 49) suggestion that 'the power equivalents of the same relative income spread show a much wider range when the underlying average income is low that when it is high,' we hypothesize that higher per capita income leads to less power inequality.

Other power-relevant variables, represented by the vector X, include race, gender, ethnicity, and the political framework through which income and other attributes are mapped to power. In the present analysis, race and ethnicity are of particular interest, as the gender composition of the population varies little from state to state, and all states operate within the broad political framework based on the US Constitution.

Accordingly, our econometric model of the determinants of power inequality is:

$$\Pi = \alpha_1 + \beta_1 G + \beta_2 Y + \beta_3 RACE + \beta_4 ETH + \delta_j RD_j + \mu_1 \qquad (6.1a)$$

where G is the Gini ratio of income distribution and Y is per capita income (both refer to pre-tax income). *RACE* is the percentage of African-Americans in the state's population; *ETH* is the percentage of people of Hispanic origin; RD_j are dummy variables that partition the country into four regions to allow for regional differences not captured in the other variables; and μ_1 is an independent, normally distributed error term with zero mean.

A poor fit in the estimation of equation (6.1a) would suggest that our power distribution measure is flawed, or that our hypotheses as to its determinants are incorrect, or both. A good fit, by contrast, would support our analysis on both counts.

Power Distribution and Environmental Policy

The beneficiaries of pollution-generating activities include producers and consumers. Producers receive what Templet (1995: 143) terms a 'pollution subsidy,' consisting of dollars not spent on pollution control, and consumers reap part of this subsidy via lower prices. In welfare-analytic terms, these benefits accrue via producers' surplus and consumers' surplus. These activities impose external costs on those adversely affected by the pollution. For some individuals, the benefits of the pollution-generating activity exceed the costs. For others, the costs are likely to exceed the benefits.

As in Chapter 5, let b_i represent the net benefit to the ith individual (net cost if $b_i < 0$) from the pollution-generating economic activity. The normative policy-making rule of benefit-cost analysis is to set the level of pollution so as to maximize aggregate net benefits, that is:

$$\max_i \sum b_i$$

Given declining marginal benefits and rising marginal costs, this rule yields the standard efficiency condition: the optimal level of pollution is defined as the point where the marginal social benefit of an additional unit of the pollution-generating activity equals its marginal social cost.

Again, as in Chapters 4 and 5, let us hypothesize that actual policy outcomes are better described by a 'power-weighted social decision rule' (PWSDR):

$$\max_i \sum \pi_i b_i$$

where π_i = the power of the ith individual. 'Power' here plays the same role as 'influence' in Becker's (1983) model of the determination of fiscal policy. Instead of maximizing net benefits, social decisions maximize net benefits weighted by the power of the individuals to whom they accrue.

The positive PWSDR corresponds to the normative benefit-cost rule only in the special case in which all individuals have equal power. When the power of those who benefit from pollution-generating activities exceeds the power of those who bear net costs (that is, when b_i is positively correlated with π_i), the PWSDR predicts inefficiently high levels of pollution. Conversely, when the beneficiaries are less powerful than those who bear net costs (that is, b_i is negatively correlated with π_i), the PWSDR predicts 'excessive' pollution control, in the sense that the marginal social benefit of the pollution-generating activity exceeds its marginal social cost. In the former case, greater power inequality results in more pollution; in the latter, less. In both cases, power inequality drives a wedge between the social costs and benefits of externality-generating activities and the weighted costs and benefits which enter into the political process of decision-making.[7]

The net environmental impact of power inequality hinges, therefore, on the correlation between the net benefits derived from pollution-generating activities (b_i) and power (π_i), summed over all pollution-generating activities. As noted in Chapters 4 and 5, there are reasonable grounds to expect this correlation to be positive. Richer individuals generally reap more producers' and consumers' surplus than do poorer individuals by virtue of the simple facts that they own more productive assets and consume more goods and services. At the same time, richer individuals tend to be more powerful, insofar as purchasing power confers effective demand in 'political markets.' For these reasons we hypothesize that those who receive the greatest net benefits from pollution-generating economic activities will tend, in general, to be relatively powerful. Conversely, those who bear the greatest net costs will tend to be less powerful. If so, the PWSDR predicts that greater power inequality will lead, on balance, to higher levels of pollution.

Again, this is not to say that rich and powerful individuals are not concerned about pollution nor less concerned than anyone else. Indeed, clean air and clean water are quite likely to be 'normal' goods – that is, individual demand for them (measured by willingness to pay) rises with income. The extent to which this demand translates into less pollution is limited, however, by two factors in addition to the well-known free-rider problem. First, clean air and clean water are not pure public goods: those who can afford to do so can reside in relatively unpolluted enclaves, drink bottled water, vacation in pristine locations, and in these and other ways purchase private insulation from public bads. Second, against any greater preference among higher-income individuals for the public-good dimensions of environmental quality, we must weigh their higher price in terms of forgone benefits.

We hypothesize, therefore, that environmental policies will tend to be weaker where power inequality is greater:

$$EP = f(\Pi, Z), f_\Pi < 0 \tag{6.2}$$

where EP is an index of environmental policy weakness (that is, a higher value denotes weaker policies); Π is a measure of the distribution of power (where a higher value denotes a more equal distribution); and Z is a vector of other determinants of environmental policies. Three other environmental policy determinants are included in our analysis: the manufacturing share of output (MAN), urbanization (URB), and population density (PD). Each of these is expected to generate demand for stronger environmental policies.

Hence we will estimate the following econometric equation:

$$EP = \alpha_2 + \gamma_1 \Pi + \gamma_2 MAN + \gamma_3 URB + \gamma_4 PD + \mu_2 \tag{6.2a}$$

where μ_2 is again an independent, normally distributed error term with zero mean.

Environmental Policy and Environmental Stress

Weaker environmental policies are expected to lead to greater environmental stress. The next equation tests for this impact:

$$ES = \alpha_3 + \delta_1 EP + \delta_2 MAN + \delta_3 URB + \delta_4 PD + \mu_3 \qquad (6.3)$$

where *ES* is an index of environmental stress (a higher value denoting greater stress) and μ_3 is an error term with the usual properties. This equation again includes manufacturing, urbanization, and population density as control variables on the right-hand side, since these are expected to lead to greater environmental stress independently of the environmental policies. We test for endogeneity of *EP* in eq. (6.3) to examine the possibility that after controlling for these variables greater environmental stress leads to stronger environmental policies (a relationship which would tend to mask the effect of policy on stress).[8]

Environmental Stress and Public Health

The impact of environmental stress on public health is estimated by a final link in the recursive chain:

$$HEALTH = \alpha_4 + \Phi_1 ES + \Phi_2 \Pi + \mu_4 \qquad (6.4)$$

where *HEALTH* is a measure of public health and μ_4 an error term with the usual properties. We include our power distribution measure on the right-hand side to allow for the possibility that it may affect public health by other avenues apart from environmental stress. Three alternative measures of *HEALTH* are used: infant mortality (*IM*), the premature death rate (*PDR*), and a composite public health index (*PHI*).

Figure 6.1 summarizes the structure of our model. In addition to the causal linkages specified here, it is conceivable that environmental policies and outcomes in turn affect the determinants of power inequality. For example, it is sometimes asserted that environmental regulation acts as a brake on economic growth, which over time could lead to lower per capita incomes. It is doubtful, however, that such effects have been either strong enough or rapid enough to have had much effect on the existing income disparities among states.[9] Environmental policies could also affect income inequality. Templet (1995), for example, argues that pollution subsidies (consisting of unspent pollution control dollars) accrue disproportionately to the higher-income classes. In this chapter, we confine our attention to the causal relations depicted in Figure 6.1, on the assumption that power in-

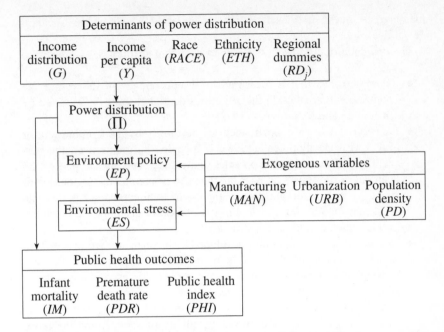

Figure 6.1   The power–environment–health model summarized

equality is a largely exogenous determinant of environmental policies and outcomes.

DATA

This section derives our measure of interstate variations in the distribution of power, and discusses the other data used in our analysis. Descriptive statistics for all the variables are presented in Table 6.A1.

A Measure of Power Distribution

Our measure of interstate variations in power distribution is based on the premise that voter participation, tax fairness, Medicaid accessibility, and educational attainment levels have something in common: higher levels of these four variables reflect a more equal distribution of power, and lower levels a more unequal distribution. We use the method of principal components to estimate statistically this common feature, here defined as the first principal component of this set of variables (which are standardized, that is, measured as the deviations from the means and divided by the standard deviations).

The raw data for construction of this measure are as follows:

- *Voter participation* is measured by the percentage of the voting age population that voted in the 1992 Presidential election, as reported by Scammon and McGillvray (1993).
- *Tax fairness* is a composite measure developed by the Corporation for Enterprise Development (1995). It includes information on the percentage of income spent on sales and excise taxes by the poorest 20 percent of the state's population, the ratio of the income tax burden of the top 1 percent of taxpayers to that of the bottom 60 percent, the state personal income tax threshold, and corporate tax policies. A higher value indicates a fairer tax structure.
- *Medicaid access* is an index developed by Erdman and Wolfe (1987) to assess interstate differences in poor people's access to health care through the Medicaid program. We regard this as a proxy for the degree of power inequality on the expenditure side of state fiscal policy. The index is based on eligibility restrictions, the scope of services, the availability of healthcare providers, quality of service, and the reimbursement system. A higher value indicates greater access.
- *Educational attainment* is measured by the percentage of the state's population aged 25 years and older that has at minimum graduated from high school according to the 1990 Census of Population (US Department of Commerce 1995: 159).

Our measure of power distribution (Π), derived from these four variables, is reported in Table 6.1.[10] Its mean is zero; a higher value indicates a more equal distribution of power. Minnesota has the most equal distribution of power among the 50 states by this measure, and Mississippi the most unequal distribution. There is a striking regional pattern in that the Southern states display the greatest inequality.

Determinants of Power Inequality

Power distribution is expected to be negatively related to the Gini ratio of income distribution, race, and ethnicity, and positively related to per capita income.

The *Gini ratio of income distribution* and *per capita income* are calculated from the US Census Bureau's Current Population Survey (CPS) data for 1991–3.[11] Both variables refer to pre-tax income. A higher Gini ratio indicates greater income inequality.

Table 6.1 Interstate variations in the distribution of power

Minnesota	2.32	Rhode Island	−0.08
Maine	1.65	Pennsylvania	−0.10
Wisconsin	1.42	Arizona	−0.12
Vermont	1.36	Delaware	−0.16
Montana	1.31	Wyoming	−0.40
Oregon	1.22	Missouri	−0.45
Connecticut	1.13	South Dakota	−0.49
Idaho	0.99	Hawaii	−0.53
Colorado	0.99	Oklahoma	−0.64
Utah	0.98	Virginia	−0.64
Nebraska	0.93	Indiana	−0.66
Alaska	0.90	New Mexico	−0.69
Massachusetts	0.81	Florida	−0.89
Kansas	0.79	Nevada	−0.91
California	0.77	Louisiana	−0.94
North Dakota	0.68	Kentucky	−1.08
Iowa	0.68	North Carolina	−1.11
New Hampshire	0.59	South Carolina	−1.19
Maryland	0.39	Georgia	−1.19
Illinois	0.38	West Virginia	−1.28
Michigan	0.36	Texas	−1.41
Washington	0.27	Arkansas	−1.50
New Jersey	0.26	Tennessee	−1.52
New York	0.22	Alabama	−1.61
Ohio	−0.07	Mississippi	−1.74

Note: Higher value denotes a more equal distribution of power. For method of calculation, see text.

Race and *ethnicity* are measured by the percentage of the state's population classified as black and Hispanic, respectively, by the Bureau of the Census in 1990, calculated from data reported by the US Department of Commerce (1992).

The regional dummy variables partition the states into four regions – the Northeast, Midwest, South, and West – following the classification used by the US Department of Commerce in its annual *Statistical Abstract of the United States*.

Indexes of Environmental Policy and Environmental Stress

The *environmental policy index* is a composite measure based on 77 indicators reported by Hall and Kerr (1991: 5). Its components include: the existence of state policies on recycling, landfills, toxic waste management, air pollution, water quality, agriculture, energy, and transportation; ratings of state environmental programs; state spending on environmental programs; and Congressional leadership on environmental issues.[12] The index is reported in Table 6.2. A lower score indicates stronger environmental policies; according

Table 6.2   The environmental policy index

California	764	Colorado	2330
Oregon	1096	Indiana	2332
New Jersey	1150	Kansas	2478
Connecticut	1225	Georgia	2505
Maine	1246	Nebraska	2510
Wisconsin	1261	Montana	2533
Minnesota	1305	South Carolina	2537
New York	1346	Kentucky	2625
Massachusetts	1377	Louisiana	2644
Rhode Island	1384	Texas	2659
Michigan	1552	Idaho	2708
Vermont	1578	North Dakota	2762
Florida	1604	New Mexico	2798
Washington	1606	Arizona	2802
Maryland	1660	Tennessee	2843
Iowa	1841	Utah	2888
Illinois	1865	Oklahoma	2913
North Carolina	1873	Nevada	2917
Ohio	2010	Wyoming	2924
New Hampshire	2054	West Virginia	2951
Pennsylvania	2058	Mississippi	3016
Virginia	2181	Alaska	3043
Missouri	2182	South Dakota	3154
Hawaii	2239	Alabama	3212
Delaware	2261	Arkansas	3230

Note: A higher score indicates weaker environmental policies.

Source: Hall and Kerr (1991: 5).

to this index, California has the strongest environmental policies among the 50 states and Arkansas the weakest.

The *environmental stress index* is a composite measure based on 167 indicators reported by Hall and Kerr (1991).[13] The components include measures of air pollution, water pollution, energy use and production, transportation efficiency, toxic chemical releases, hazardous and solid waste production, workplace conditions, agricultural pollution, and the state of forestry and fishery resources. The index is reported in Table 6.3. A higher score indicates greater environmental stress; according to this index, Ver-

Table 6.3   The environmental stress index

Vermont	3118	Delaware	4235
Hawaii	3159	Nebraska	4277
Oregon	3169	Oklahoma	4373
Nevada	3334	Florida	4402
Maine	3374	New Jersey	4420
South Dakota	3411	South Carolina	4451
Rhode Island	3473	Missouri	4461
Idaho	3473	Michigan	4464
New Hampshire	3520	Iowa	4501
Massachusetts	3562	North Carolina	4505
Minnesota	3575	Virginia	4538
Colorado	3576	Pennsylvania	4578
Washington	3623	Georgia	4598
Maryland	3679	Kentucky	4643
Montana	3688	Arkansas	4711
Alaska	3709	West Virginia	4726
New York	3785	Mississippi	4774
North Dakota	3805	Illinois	4839
New Mexico	3850	Tennessee	4928
California	3965	Alabama	4976
Wisconsin	4016	Kansas	5057
Utah	4065	Ohio	5072
Connecticut	4126	Texas	5195
Arizona	4207	Louisiana	5261
Wyoming	4228	Indiana	5279

Note: A higher score indicates greater environmental stress.

Source: Calculated from data in Hall and Kerr (1991: 5, 90).

mont has the least environmental stress among the 50 states, and Indiana the most.

Control Variables

Three variables are included as controls in the environmental policy and environmental stress equations: the manufacturing share of output, urbanization, and population density. These are expected to lead, *ceteris paribus*, to stronger environmental policies and to greater environmental stress.

The *manufacturing share of output* is the percentage share of manufactured goods in the state's gross domestic product in 1991, calculated from data reported by the US Department of Commerce (1995: 455).

Urbanization refers to the percentage of the state's total population residing in metropolitan areas in 1990, as reported by the US Department of Commerce (1992: 29).

Population density is the number of inhabitants per square mile in 1990, as reported by the US Department of Commerce (1992: 23).

Health Outcomes

Three health measures are used in our final set of equations, permitting us to examine the sensitivity of the results to different specifications of the dependent variable.

The *premature death rate* refers to the rate per 1000 people who died before age 65 due to illness or injury, as calculated from 1986 US Public Health Service data by the Northwestern National Life Insurance Company and reported by Hall and Kerr (1991: 89).

The *infant mortality rate* refers to deaths of infants under 1 year of age per 1000 live births in the year 1991, as reported by the National Center for Health Statistics (US Department of Commerce 1994).

The *public health index* is a composite measure based on 23 indicators reported by Morgan *et al.* (1994). In addition to infant mortality and the overall death rate, index components include death rates from specific causes, the percentage of low birthweight babies, and other variables not directly influenced by environmental stress such as the percentage of children immunized at age 2, the percentage of the population covered by health insurance, and the extent of alcohol consumption and smoking. The index is the average of the sum of state rankings; a higher value indicates better public health.

ECONOMETRIC RESULTS

To assess the validity of the measure of power distribution and in an effort to gain some insight into its determinants, we first estimated eq. (6.1a) by ordinary least squares (OLS), with and without the regional dummy variables. The results are presented in Table 6.4. Regional dummy variables are included for the South, Midwest, and West; hence the intercept term refers to the Northeast, and the coefficients on the dummy variables indicate the intercept shift for the other regions.[14]

Table 6.4   Regression results: determinants of power distribution

	Excluding regional dummies	Including regional dummies
Gini	-13.63^*	-11.62
(*G*)	(2.02)	(1.74)
Income	$5.03 \times 10^{-2*}$	2.82×10^{-2}
(*Y*)	(2.60)	(1.32)
Black	$-4.70 \times 10^{-2*}$	-1.84×10^{-2}
(*RACE*)	(3.52)	(1.09)
Hispanic	-0.98×10^{-2}	-1.22×10^{-2}
(*ETH*)	(0.62)	(0.76)
Intercept	3.52	3.79
	(1.26)	(1.32)
South		-1.00^*
		(2.57)
Midwest		-0.13
		(0.40)
West		-0.13
		(0.41)
Adjusted R^2	0.52	0.57

Notes:
* denotes statistical significance at 5% level.
Absolute *t*-ratios in parentheses.

The adjusted coefficients of multiple determination, 0.52 without the regional dummy variables and 0.57 with them, indicate that the model 'explains' more than half of the variation in power distribution. In each regression the estimated coefficients on the Gini ratio, per capita income, race, and ethnicity have the expected signs: higher income inequality and higher percentages of black and Hispanic minorities are associated with a less equal distribution of power, and higher per capita income with a more equal distribution. The estimated coefficients on the Gini ratio, income, and race are statistically significant at the 5 percent level. The statistical significance of these coefficients diminishes when the regional dummies are included, but their signs remain unchanged, suggesting that the variables are not simply acting as proxies for omitted region-related variables.[15] Further, the test for the joint irrelevance of the three regional dummy variables was insignificant at the 5 percent level.[16] These results suggest that our measure successfully captures interstate variations in the distribution of power. The results are consistent with the hypothesis that income distribution, per capita income, race, and ethnicity are important determinants of the distribution of power in the United States.

OLS estimation of eq. (6.2a), analyzing the determinants of environmental policy, gave the following result (absolute t-ratios in parentheses):

$$EP = 3430.9 - 395.85\,\Pi - 24.15MAN - 10.29URB - 0.74PD \qquad (6.5)$$
$$(14.29)\quad(6.99)\quad(2.86)\qquad(3.17)\qquad(2.46)$$

$$\overline{R}^2 = 0.66$$

The model 'explains' about two-thirds of the variance in the environmental policy index. The estimated coefficient on the power distribution measure has the expected sign and is statistically significant at the 0.01 percent level, a result consistent with our hypothesis that greater inequality in the distribution of power is associated with weaker environmental policies. The coefficients on the three control variables also have the expected signs; those on manufacturing and urbanization are statistically significant at the 1 percent level, and the coefficient on population density is statistically significant at the 5 percent level.

OLS estimation of equation (6.3) provides evidence that environmental policy in turn has a statistically significant impact on environmental stress:

$$ES = 1319.7 + 0.56EP + 55.60MAN + 9.84URB - 0.04PD \qquad (6.6)$$
$$(2.98)\quad(4.98)\qquad(6.00)\qquad(2.70)\qquad(0.10)$$

$$\overline{R}^2 = 0.51$$

The model again performs well, 'explaining' roughly half the variance in the environmental stress index. The estimated coefficient on environmental policy has the expected sign and is statistically significant at the 0.01 percent level, as is the estimated coefficient on manufacturing. The urbanization coefficient is statistically significant at the 1 percent level. Population density, however, appears to have no statistically significant independent impact on interstate variations in environmental stress. A Hausman (1978) test for endogeneity of the environmental policy index was negative.

Finally, Table 6.5 presents the results of OLS regressions of eq. (6.4), in which the dependent variables are three measures of public health outcomes. The results indicate that environmental stress is associated with higher infant mortality rates, higher premature death rates, and lower scores on the composite public health index. In the simple regressions, the estimated coefficients on the environmental stress index are statistically significant at the 0.01 percent level. When the power distribution measure is also included on the right-hand side its estimated coefficients are statistically significant at the 0.01 percent level; the statistical significance of the estimated coefficients on the environmental stress index diminishes but they retain the expected sign. These results suggest that environmental stress has serious adverse impacts on public health, and that power inequality has additional adverse impacts apart from those mediated by environmental policy and environmental stress.[17]

To summarize, the econometric results are consistent with the set of causal linkages hypothesized in our recursive model. Income inequality, per capita income, race and ethnicity affect power distribution in the expected directions. A more equal distribution of power is associated with stronger environmental policies, and these in turn are associated with lower environmental stress. Both environmental stress and power inequality are associated with adverse public health outcomes.

CONCLUSIONS AND IMPLICATIONS FOR POLICY

These results provide further empirical support to the hypothesis that greater power inequality leads to greater environmental degradation. Disparities of power appear to affect not only the distribution of the net costs and benefits of environmentally degrading activities, but also the overall *magnitude* of environmental degradation. In addition, our results are consistent with the hypothesis that income, income inequality, race, and ethnicity are among the determinants of the distribution of power in the USA. The impacts of environmental stress and power inequality on public health underscore the policy relevance of these findings: for some Americans, the linkages identified here are literally a matter of life and death.

The methodology developed here can assist policy makers in identifying those states most likely to benefit from Federal environmental enforcement assistance. As state responsibility for the implementation of environmental mandates increases, the importance of such information is increasing.[18] If complete and accurate environmental data were available, the identification

Table 6.5 Regression results: determinants of public health outcomes

Variable	Infant mortality (*IM*)		Premature death rate (*PDR*)		Public health index (*PHI*)	
Intercept	2.93*	5.65*	7.16*	11.40*	46.01*	33.76*
	(2.37)	(4.16)	(5.27)	(8.88)	(11.90)	(9.37)
Environmental stress (*ES*)	$1.40 \times 10^{-3*}$	$7.52 \times 10^{-4*}$	$1.40 \times 10^{-3*}$	3.88×10^{-4}	$-5.04 \times 10^{-3*}$	$-2.10 \times 10^{-3*}$
	(4.79)	(2.33)	(4.35)	(1.27)	(5.49)	(2.45)
Power distribution (Π)		-0.68*		-1.07*		3.09*
		(3.49)		(5.76)		(5.93)
Adjusted R^2	0.31	0.44	0.27	0.56	0.37	0.63

Notes:
* denotes statistical significance at 5% level.
Absolute *t*-ratios in parentheses.

problem would not exist: environmental protection needs could be assessed directly. The inadequacy of such data, however, is a fundamental part of the enforcement problem – hence the need for diagnostic tools for drawing inferences from other data.

Our findings suggest that Federal enforcement resources can have the greatest impact in states with relatively unequal distributions of power, and that the latter can be estimated from available data. Further refinements – including the analysis of specific subsets of environmental variables, the development of other power-distribution indicators, and studies of interstate variations within particular geographic regions – potentially could enhance the usefulness and strengthen the predictive power of this methodology.

The broader implication of our analysis is that democratization – in its broad sense, meaning movement toward a more equitable distribution of power – can foster environmental protection. This suggests that democracy-strengthening measures – including public participation, right-to-know laws, and accountability to local communities – are important elements of environmental policy. Such measures can entail short-term costs. Public engagement can complicate the lives of decision makers, and it sometimes produces slower results than a top-down approach. Efforts to strengthen democracy can yield long-run environmental benefits, however, by redressing inequalities of power that invite pollution beyond socially desirable levels.

APPENDIX

Table 6.A1   US states: descriptive statistics

Variable	Mean	Standard deviation	Minimum	Maximum
Power distribution (Π)	0.00	1.00	−1.74	2.32
Gini coefficient (*G*)	0.37	0.02	0.33	0.42
Income per capita (*Y*)	40.46	5.73	29.27	53.28
Black (*RACE*)	9.53	9.24	0.25	35.56
Hispanic (*ETH*)	5.37	7.52	0.45	38.22
Environmental policy (*EP*)	2200.00	670.00	764.00	3230.00
Environmental stress (*ES*)	4175.00	607.00	3118.00	5279.00
Manufacturing (*MAN*)	17.39	6.71	3.00	30.40
Urbanization (*URB*)	66.74	21.68	24.00	100.00
Population density (*PD*)	166.10	235.20	1.00	1042.00
Infant mortality (*IM*)	8.79	1.50	5.80	11.80
Premature death rate (*PDR*)	13.02	1.60	9.78	16.38
Public health index (*PHI*)	24.99	4.91	17.09	35.09
Voter participation	58.30	7.31	41.90	72.00
Tax fairness	38.25	17.95	6.10	77.73
Medicaid access	56.80	9.02	38.00	75.00
Educational attainment	76.27	5.62	64.40	86.50

NOTES

We are grateful to Michael Podolsky for comments on an earlier draft of this chapter, and to Mariano Torras, José Molinas, and Nasrin Dalirazar for research assistance.

1. The populations of Chester, Pennsylvania, Louisiana's 'Cancer Alley', and South Central Los Angeles are predominantly African-American; the population of East Los Angeles is predominantly Hispanic. See Janofsky (1996), Bullard (1990), and Kay (1991) for details. See Cole (1992: 621–34), Been (1993: 1009–13), and Bullard (1994) for further examples.
2. Subsequent studies have demonstrated the sensitivity of these results to the geographic unit of analysis (Anderton *et al.* 1994), and have observed that these correlations may also reflect movements of minority and low-income populations in response to the effects of locally undesirable land uses on property values (Been 1994).
3. See Chapter 5 for a test using international data.
4. In analyses of the siting of hazardous waste facilities and toxic air pollution, respectively, Hamilton (1993) and Brooks and Sethi (1997) take voter turnout as a measure of the propensity of communities to engage in collective action. At the state level, voter turnout

similarly can be interpreted as a measure of the propensity of less powerful social classes to engage in collective action *vis-à-vis* the more powerful, on the assumptions that the less powerful are (a) less likely to vote and (b) less able to influence the political process by other means (for example, via financial contributions).

5. One way in which information may affect environmental outcomes is via effects on preferences. For discussion, see Chapter 4.

6. Insofar as greater power inequality in turn leads to greater income inequality, the two are mutually reinforcing.

7. In his analysis of the siting of commercial hazardous waste facilities, Hamilton (1993: 122) observes: 'In the "Coase theorem," a firm generating externalities will locate where, *ceteris paribus*, its social damage will be the least, because that is where potential compensation is the least. Yet the differing degree to which groups organize to demand compensation and raise a firm's costs of choosing a particular location drives a wedge between the social costs of its externalities and the costs voiced through the political process of its site selection.' Here we regard 'the differing degree to which groups organize,' and differences in the efficacy of their efforts, as reflections of their power *vis-à-vis* others.

8. Stronger environmental policies (here denoted by a lower value of *EP*) are expected to lead to lower environmental stress; therefore, in equation (6.3) we expect $\delta_1 > 0$. If greater environmental stress led to stronger environmental policies, this would downwardly bias our estimate of δ_1. Such endogeneity would therefore increase the risk of a Type I error (rejection of the true hypothesis that stronger policies lead to lower stress), but would lower the risk of a Type II error (mistaken acceptance of the hypothesis).

9. Meyer (1995) examines state-level data and finds no systematic relationship between state environmental policies and state economic performance. Some studies have found negative relationships between environmental regulatory stringency and selected measures of economic activity (notably new plant locations and business start-ups), but the estimated effects tend to be small. For a review of these studies, see Tannenwald (1997).

10. The measure's correlations with the four variables from which it is extracted are: voter participation 0.76, tax fairness 0.79, Medicaid access 0.68, and educational attainment 0.80.

11. We are grateful to John Haveman of Purdue University for providing us with calculations of the Gini ratio and per capita income based on the CPS data.

12. The index is derived by ranking the states from 1 to 50 for each indicator and then summing the rankings. A limitation of this measure is that it is based on ordinal rather than cardinal information: one would ideally like to know not only that policy *x* is weaker in state A than in state B, but also how much weaker. A second limitation is that all 77 policies are given equal weight, despite the fact that some may be more important than others, and that their relative importance may vary from state to state. The comprehensiveness of the measure dampens noise in the rankings for the individual indicators. Meyer (1993) reports a fairly strong correlation ($r = 0.72$) between this index and an earlier one developed by Duerksen (1983), suggesting that it provides a reasonably robust measure.

13. Hall and Kerr (1991: 5) present a composite 'green conditions index' based on 179 indicators. Our environmental stress index is recalculated by dropping 12 community health indicators, since we wish to examine public health outcomes separately.

14. Tests for heteroscedasticity, including White's test (White 1980), were carried out for these and the other regressions reported below; in no case did these reject the null hypothesis of homoscedastic error terms.

15. The relatively low t-ratios in the second regression, coupled with the R^2, reflect multicollinearity; in particular, there is a strong correlation between *RACE* and the dummy variable for the South ($r = 0.72$).

16. The calculated test statistic was 2.75, less than the critical value of the F-statistic of 2.83.

17. The latter finding is consistent with recent studies linking income distribution to mortality in the US; see Kaplan *et al.* (1996) and Kennedy *et al.* (1996).

18. In November 1996 the US Environmental Protection Agency's top enforcement official called for a nationwide effort to determine the extent of under-reporting of serious environmental violations by state governmental agencies (Cushman 1996).

REFERENCES

Anderton, D.L., Anderson, A.B., Rossi, P.H., Oakes, J.M., Fraser, M.R., Weber, E.W. and Calabrese, E.J. (1994), 'Hazardous waste facilities: "Environmental equity" issues in metropolitan areas,' *Evaluation Review*, 18(2): 123–40.

Becker, G.A. (1983), 'A theory of competition among pressure groups for political influence', *Quarterly Journal of Economics*, 98: 371–400.

Been, V. (1993), 'What's fairness got to do with it? Environmental justice and the siting of locally undesirable land uses,' *Cornell Law Review*, 78: 1001–85.

Been, V. (1994), 'Locally undesirable land uses in minority neighborhoods: Disproportionate siting or market dynamics?', *Yale Law Journal*, 103(6): 1383–422.

Brooks, N. and Sethi, R. (1997), 'The distribution of pollution: Community characteristics and exposure to air toxics', *Journal of Environmental Economics and Management*, 32: 233–50.

Bullard, R.D. (1983), 'Solid waste sites and the Black Houston community', *Sociological Inquiry*, 53: 273–88.

Bullard, R.D. (1990), *Dumping in Dixie: Race, Class, and Environmental Quality*, Boulder, CO: Westview Press.

Bullard, R.D. (ed.) (1994), *Unequal Protection: Environmental Justice and Communities of Color*, San Francisco, CA: Sierra Club Books.

Cole, L.W. (1992), 'Empowerment as the key to environmental protection: The need for environmental poverty law,' *Ecology Law Quarterly*, 19(4): 619–83.

Corporation for Enterprise Development (1995), *The 1995 Development Report Card for the States*, Washington, DC: Corporation for Enterprise Development.

Cushman, J.H., Jr (1996), 'States neglecting pollution rules, White House says,' *New York Times*, 15 December: A1, A37.

Duerksen, C.J. (1983), *Environmental Regulation of Industrial Plant Siting: How to Make It Work Better*, Washington, DC: Conservation Foundation.

Erdman, K. and Wolfe, S.M. (1987), *Poor Health Care for Poor Americans: A Ranking of State Medicaid Programs*, Washington, DC: Public Citizen Health Research Group.

Hall, R. and Kerr, M.L. (1991), *1991–1992 Green Index*, Washington, DC: Island Press.

Hamilton, J.T. (1993), 'Politics and social costs: Estimating the impact of collective action on hazardous waste facilities,' *Rand Journal of Economics*, 24(1): 101–25.

Hausman, J.A. (1978), 'Specification tests in econometrics,' *Econometrica*, 46: 1251–71.

Janofsky, M. (1996), 'Suit says racial bias led to clustering of waste-processing sites,' *New York Times*, 29 May: A 13, A 15.

Kaplan, G.A., Pamuk, E.R., Lynch, J.W., Cohen, R.D. and Balfour, J.L. (1996), 'Inequality in income and mortality in the United States: Analysis of mortality and potential pathways,' *British Medical Journal*, 312: 999–1003.

Kay, J. (1991), 'Minorities bear the brunt of pollution: Latinos and Blacks living in state's "dirtiest" neighborhood,' *San Francisco Examiner*, 7 April: A1, A12.

Kennedy, B.P., Kawachi, I. and Prothrow-Smith, D. (1996), 'Income distribution and mortality: Cross sectional ecological study of the Robin Hood index in the United States,' *British Medical Journal*, 312: 1004–7.

Kuznets, S. (1963), 'Quantitative aspects of the economic growth of nations,' *Economic Development and Cultural Change*, 11 (2/II): 1–80.

Meyer, S.M. (1993), 'Environmentalism and economic prosperity: An update,' Cambridge, MA: Massachusetts Institute of Technology, Department of Political Science, mimeo.

Meyer, S.M. (1995), 'The economic impact of environmental regulation,' *Journal of Environmental Law and Practice*, 3(2): 4–15.

Morgan, K.O., Morgan, S. and Quitno, N. (eds) (1994), *Health Care Rankings 1994: Health Care in the 50 United States*, Lawrence, KS: Morgan Quitno Corporation.

Perlin, S.A., Setzer, R.W., Creason, J. and Sexton, K. (1995), 'Distribution of industrial air emissions by income and race in the United States: An approach using the Toxic Release Inventory,' *Environmental Science and Technology*, 29(1): 69–80.

Scammon, R.M. and McGillvray, A.V. (1993), *America Votes 20*, Washington, DC: Congressional Quarterly.

Tannenwald, R. (1997), 'State regulatory policy and economic development,' *New England Economic Review*, March/April: 83–99.

Templet, P.H. (1995), 'Grazing the commons: An empirical analysis of externalities, subsidies and sustainability,' *Ecological Economics*, 12: 141–59.

US Department of Commerce (1992), *Statistical Abstract of the United States 1992*, Washington, DC: Department of Commerce.

US Department of Commerce (1994), *Statistical Abstract of the United States 1994*, Washington, DC: Department of Commerce.

US Department of Commerce (1995), *Statistical Abstract of the United States 1995*, Washington, DC: Department of Commerce.

US Department of Environmental Protection (1992), *Environmental Equity: Reducing Risk For All Communities*, Report to the Administrator from the Environmental Equity Workgroup, February (draft).

US General Accounting Office (1983), *Siting of Hazardous Waste Landfills and their Correlation with Racial and Economic Status of Surrounding Communities*, Washington, DC: GAO/RCED-83-168.

White, H. (1980), 'A heteroscedasticity-consistent covariance matrix estimator and a direct test for heteroscedasticity,' *Econometrica*, 48: 817–38.

7. The globalization of market failure?

INTRODUCTION

The economic case for trade liberalization rests on its capacity to extend the reach of the market's fabled invisible hand. As trade barriers are lowered and the world market grows more integrated, producers reallocate land, labor, and capital to those economic activities in which they enjoy a comparative advantage, and away from the production of goods and services which now can be more cheaply obtained from others. The result is a larger economic pie, which in principle – if seldom in practice – can benefit all concerned.

With the globalization of the market, however, comes a globalization of market failures, due to the fact that prices do not capture 'external' costs and benefits to third parties. Say that country A produces corn more cheaply than country B, but in so doing generates more pollution. In the absence of countervailing policies, trade liberalization will cause production to shift from country B to country A, with a corresponding increase in pollution and its external costs. Similarly, if producers in country B generate higher positive externalities than those in country A – for example, via the conservation of crop genetic diversity – trade liberalization will erode the supply of these benefits. In both cases, the happy ending of a bigger pie, once the external costs and benefits are counted, no longer can be taken for granted. Whether the social gains from trade liberalization will exceed the social losses from the attendant market failures is an empirical question, one which cannot be answered by theoretical fables.

This chapter considers the impact of trade-driven market failures on sustainable agriculture. By sustainable agriculture I do not refer solely to 'traditional' farming in developing countries but also to 'modern' farming: both are important to sustaining the supply of food and fiber for current and future generations. Moreover, the boundary between them becomes increasingly fuzzy as both traditional and modern agriculture evolve and interact through time.

I focus on two important types of market failures. The first is the displacement of natural fibers by synthetic substitutes, resulting from competition in which the higher pollution costs associated with the latter are not internalized in world prices. The second is the erosion of crop genetic diversity, arising from the fact that markets do not reward farmers for their provision of this public good. The next section discusses the displacement of natural fibers by synthetics, illustrated by the competition between jute and polypropylene. The third section discusses the erosion of crop genetic diversity, illustrated by the impact of the North American Free Trade Agreement (NAFTA) on Mexican maize farmers. The final section considers some policy implications of the globalization of market failure.

NATURAL FIBERS VERSUS SYNTHETIC SUBSTITUTES: THE CASE OF BANGLADESHI JUTE

Since World War Two, renewable natural raw materials including cotton, jute, wool, sisal, and rubber have lost international markets to synthetic substitutes. Between 1963 and 1986 substitution by synthetics is estimated to have reduced the consumption of natural raw materials in the industrialized countries by almost half.[1] While the production and consumption of natural raw materials are by no means free of negative environmental impacts, the environmental costs associated with the production and consumption of synthetics typically are considerably larger.

The production of many natural raw materials is concentrated in developing countries (the 'South'), while the production of synthetic substitutes is concentrated in the industrialized countries (the 'North'). Hence the competition between natural raw materials and synthetics pits relatively clean producers in the South against relatively dirty producers in the North – the opposite of what is commonly assumed in discussions of the environmental impacts of North-South trade. The competition between jute and polypropylene is a case in point.

Jute is the second most important natural fiber in world trade after cotton. It has two main end-uses: burlap (also known as hessian) cloth and carpet backing. In recent decades, jute consumption in the industrialized countries has contracted sharply in the face of competition from synthetics. Between 1970 and 1992 the annual jute imports of North America and western Europe plummeted from 1.0 million to 52,000 metric tons (Thigpen *et al.* 1987; IJO 1993). Over the same period the real price of jute declined by roughly 70 percent.[2]

Bangladesh accounts for roughly 80 percent of world jute exports (FAO 1994: 233). With a per capita income of $220 per year, Bangladesh ranks among the poorest countries in the world. Jute-related activities in agriculture, manufacturing, and trade affect the livelihoods of about 25 million Bangladeshis – roughly a quarter of the country's population (World Bank 1992). Jute cultivation requires 50 percent more labor per hectare than rice, the principal alternative crop (Hye 1993). The decline of the international jute market therefore has hit the incomes of some of the world's poorest people.

Polypropylene (PP), the main synthetic substitute for jute, is manufactured primarily in the North, although newly industrializing countries including Korea, China, and Brazil have now entered the industry. The United States is the world's largest producer, followed by Japan (United Nations 1993). PP producers include multinational firms such as Exxon, Hoechst, Hyundai Petrochemical, and Shell (Johnson 1990).

The price advantage that has permitted PP to capture and retain the erst-while markets for jute has been fairly modest. In 1990 the wholesale price ratio of jute to synthetic cloth in New York was 1.35; its average over the preceding decade was 1.42 (World Bank 1992: 12). The incorporation of environmental costs into the prices of PP and jute could substantially alter this ratio.

The major environmental impacts of PP manufacture arise from air pollu-tion and energy consumption. Air pollutants generated in PP production include particulates, sulfur oxides, nitrogen oxides, carbon monoxide, and volatile organic compounds, total emissions of which are estimated at 127 kg per ton of PP (Tellus Institute 1992: 9T-6). In addition, PP production emits smaller amounts of other toxic air pollutants, including ammonia, benzene, biphenyl, ethylbenzene, lead, methane, toluene, and xylene (*ibid.*).

Energy use in the production of PP cloth is estimated at 84 gigajoules/ton, at least six times the energy requirement for production of jute cloth (Braungart *et al.* 1992: 89). Carbon dioxide (CO_2) emissions in the PP production proc-ess are estimated at 3.7 tons per ton of fiber (*ibid.*: 91). The long-term environmental effects of additions to atmospheric CO_2 derived from fossil carbon remain uncertain, but they include impacts on agriculture, forestry, biodiversity, and a rise in the sea level. By virtue of its low-lying deltaic terrain, Bangladesh is among the countries that stand to be most adversely affected by the latter (Pearce *et al.* 1995).

Polypropylene is not biodegradable. Its recycling potential is limited by the use of additives in the production process, and by mixture with other plastics in the collection process (leading to 'downcycling,' re-use in products of inferior quality). At the end of the product life-cycle, PP disposal therefore incurs the costs of landfill storage, incineration, or litter. As much as 6 percent of PP cloth, by weight, is comprised of chemical additives, including stabilizers, coloring pigment, and flame retardants (Braungart *et al.* 1992: 66–75). These contain heavy metals including chromium, copper, lead, nickel, and zinc, which also ultimately enter the waste stream (*ibid.*: 66).

The environmental impacts of jute production are relatively modest by comparison. Jute growers use some chemical fertilizers, but not very intensively. Most apply no pesticides at all to the crop. The flooded fields in which jute ripens support diverse fish populations, which play a critical role in the Bangladeshi diet (especially in the diets of the poor). Hence the fact that jute can be grown without reliance on pesticides is an important environmental plus.

Like all plants, jute absorbs CO_2 from the atmosphere when it grows and returns it when it decays. Atmospheric CO_2 is the most important of the greenhouse gases implicated in global warming. Jute thus provides a temporary environmental benefit: it sequesters carbon while in use. The transport and milling of the fiber and the production and transport of inputs for the crop generate some CO_2 emissions, but these amount to less than one-sixth of those generated in PP manufacture (*ibid.*: 89–90).

The most serious negative environmental impacts of jute production probably arise in the process known as retting, when the jute stalks are submerged for 3–4 weeks in ponds where anaerobic microbial decomposition loosens the fiber in the inner bark. Retting causes transitory deterioration in water quality, including oxygen depletion, which can harm gill-breathing fish. The decomposition products are non-toxic, however, and these enhance soil fertility (Alam 1993: 362). Retting releases methane, a potent greenhouse gas, in quantities which have yet to be measured; technologies to capture the methane for use as biogas fuel are still at an experimental stage.

Environmental impacts in the manufacturing stage of jute production arise primarily from energy consumption, the production of fiber wastes, and pollution from dyes. Energy use in jute production is estimated at up to 14 gigajoules/ton (Braungart *et al.* 1992: 89). Jute dust waste produced during processing amounts to roughly 2 percent of the fiber; some of this is burned for energy (*ibid.*: 35). Only a small fraction of jute fabrics – around 1 to 2 percent – is dyed, but effluent samples from jute dyeing processes show releases of heavy metals (*ibid.*: 34, 39).

Jute is biodegradable: at the end of the product life-cycle it decomposes in the soil. Residues from mineral oils used to soften the fiber may persist; conversion to the use of vegetable oils for this purpose would ensure rapid and complete biodegradation (*ibid.*: 38).

Several further positive side-effects of jute warrant mention. The edible leaves of the plant provide a cheap (often free) source of food for the poor, and the jute stalks, left after the fiber is stripped away, are a renewable source of cooking fuel and building material. The high labor intensity of jute cultivation also can be regarded as a social benefit in a land where agricultural laborers are among the poorest of the world's poor.

To date there have been no comprehensive attempts to evaluate the full range of environmental impacts of jute and PP in economic terms. Elsewhere (Boyce 1995), however, I have performed exploratory valuations for three

Table 7.1   Effect of internalization of environmental costs on relative price of jute and polypropylene

	Prices ($/000 yd^2)		Price ratio (jute/PP)
	Jute	PP	
Market price (1990)	240	178	1.35
Prices internalizing PP air pollution costs only	240	224	1.07
Prices internalizing CO$_2$ costs only	242	182	1.33
Prices internalizing non-biodegradable disposal costs only	240	180	1.33
Prices internalizing all of the above	242	230	1.05

Source: Boyce (1995).

major impacts: air pollution, carbon dioxide emissions, and solid waste disposal. Table 7.1 summarizes the results, showing how internalization of these costs would affect the relative price of jute and polypropylene.

Air pollution has the greatest impact. The calculations in Table 7.1 include only the high-volume pollutants (particulates, sulfur oxides, nitrogen oxides, carbon monoxide, and volatile organics), and not the other toxic air pollutants released in smaller quantities in PP manufacture. The monetary values used to translate these emissions into costs are derived from the average values adopted by policy-making agencies in the United States as a whole; these are considerably below those used in densely populated and highly polluted regions such as southern California. Carbon dioxide emissions are here valued at $50 per ton of carbon.[3] No account is taken of the positive benefit provided by carbon sequestration in jute, on the grounds that in the long run this carbon returns to the atmosphere via biodegradation. Disposal costs at the end of the product life cycle are based on average tipping fees at landfills in the United States.[4]

A more complete analysis of the environmental costs of jute and PP would incorporate other impacts, including the effects of fertilizer runoff and retting on water quality in the case of jute; the impact of methane emissions during jute retting; the impacts of the heavy metals and other chemical additives used in the manufacturing processes of PP and jute; and the impact of other toxic air pollutants emitted in PP production. If, as seems likely, the most economically important of these are the costs associated with emissions of toxic pollutants – due to the use of chemical additives (the quantity of which is greater in PP) and due to the other air pollutants released in PP production

– then internalization of these costs would further lower the jute/PP price ratio.

The price advantage that has enabled polypropylene to displace jute so dramatically in world markets therefore rests, in no small measure, on the failure of market prices to reflect environmental costs. Correction of this market failure would benefit not only the global environment, but also some of the world's poorest people, the jute growers and agricultural laborers of Bangladesh. The absence of corrective policies, on the other hand, benefits some of the world's largest corporations. The paucity of international attention to the environmental implications of the displacement of natural fibers by synthetics may reflect the power disparities between their producers.

GENETIC DIVERSITY: THE CASE OF MEXICAN MAIZE

Some five millennia ago, the ancestors of the Mayan farmers in what are now Mexico and Guatemala achieved what must rank among the great technological advances of history, in terms of its cumulative impact on human well-being: the domestication of maize. Over time, the cultivation of maize spread among the indigenous peoples of the Americas and, with the arrival of the Europeans, it would spread across the globe. Yet the crop's historic center of origin has remained its center of genetic diversity, in keeping with the association first postulated in the 1920s by the great Russian botanist N.I. Vavilov (1992).

No worldwide inventory of genetic diversity in maize (or other crops) exists. An indicator of its geographical distribution, however, can be derived from the holdings of the world's most comprehensive gene banks. The number of accessions from a given country, normalized for differences in acreage, provides a rough index of genetic diversity. Although not a perfect measure – gene-bank collections are uneven across countries and some accessions are duplicates – this can provide a useful first approximation.

Table 7.2 presents data on accessions held at the world's premier maize research institute, the International Center for Maize and Wheat Improvement (CIMMYT) near Mexico City. Mexico accounts for about one-third of the gene bank's 13,000 holdings, and the country ranks highest on the diversity index. Guatemala, with only 2.5 percent of the maize acreage of the United States, accounts for almost 14 times as many varieties.

Scientists call the hilly, rain-fed maize plots of south-central Mexico and Guatemala 'evolutionary gardens,' or 'gardens of chaos' (Wilkes 1992). Here the maize plant continues to evolve under the full pressure of natural selection. As the climate changes, and as new strains of insect pests and plant diseases evolve, the interaction between nature and human purpose in these plots yields a stream of new varieties adapted to the new conditions. The

Table 7.2   Maize diversity in selected countries

Country	Number of accessions at CIMMYT	Maize acreage (1992–4 average, '000 ha)	Genetic diversity index[a]
Mexico	4220	7536	289.8
Brazil	2508	12992	146.3
Guatemala	590	709	82.4
Argentina	152	2430	14.7
United States	43	28047	2.0
China	25	20821	1.3
India	4	6052	0.3
Philippines	3	3240	0.3
Nigeria	1	1567	0.1

Note: [a] Genetic diversity index = $V/A^{0.3}$, where V = number of accessions and A = acreage.

Source: Boyce (1996).

campesino (peasant) farmers of the region thus not only maintain a vast stock of maize varieties, but also manage an ongoing flow of new varieties.

Maize is the number one crop in Mexico and the United States. In the USA it covers one-seventh of the arable land; in Mexico nearly one-third. With average yields of 7.4 metric tons per hectare (mt/ha), the USA produces roughly 200 million mt of maize annually on roughly 300,000 farms. Mexico, with average yields of 2.0 mt/ha, produces roughly 14 million mt on 2.7 million farms (see Table 7.3). Most US maize is used as animal feed; most Mexican maize is consumed directly by humans.

US production techniques differ dramatically from those of the Mexican *campesinos*. Half a dozen varieties account for almost half of the US maize acreage, and only a few hundred, many of them closely related, are available commercially. With so large an area under so few varieties, the US maize crop is highly vulnerable to insect and disease epidemics, as was dramatically illustrated when leaf blight destroyed one-fifth of the nation's harvest in 1970 (Walsh 1981). To keep ahead of rapidly evolving pests, plant breeders must release a constant stream of new varieties; for this reason, the average commercial lifespan of a maize variety in the US is only seven years (Duvick 1984: 164). The ultimate raw material for this varietal relay race is the maize germplasm originating from the evolutionary gardens of traditional agriculture.[5]

Herbicides are used on 96 percent of US maize acreage, and insecticides on about one-third. Comparable data are not available for Mexico, but pesti-

Table 7.3   Corn agriculture in Mexico and the United States

	Mexico	United States
Production		
Area (million hectares)	7.3	27.1
Share in total cropland (%)	31.7	14.4
Yield (metric tons/ha)	2.0	7.4
Output (million mt)	14.6	201.5
Number of farms (million)	2.7	0.3
Input use		
Area fertilized (%)	70	97
Area under hybrids (%)	33	100
Area irrigated (%)	15	80
Area treated with herbicides (%)	n.a.	96
Area treated with insecticides (%)	n.a.	29
Tractors/farm worker	0.02	1.5
Varietal diversity		
Number of varieties available	5000	454
Share of top six varieties (% of area)	n.a.	43

Note: n.a. = not available.

Source: Boyce (1996).

cide usage in maize farming there is considerably lower, particularly among small farmers.[6] The herbicides and insecticides applied to US maize have resulted in widespread contamination of groundwater. A survey conducted by the US Environmental Protection Agency (1990) found that atrazine, the most widely used herbicide in corn fields, was present in the water of one in every 60 community water systems and in one in 140 private wells nationwide.[7]

By the price standard of the market, the US produces maize more 'efficiently' than Mexico. When NAFTA was being negotiated, US maize cost about $110 per ton at the border, while in Mexico maize farmers received $240 per ton (Scott 1992). The Mexican government has long restricted maize imports to protect domestic farmers. This protection is now being phased out over a 15-year period under the terms of NAFTA. The controversial nature of this move within Mexico is reflected by the fact that this is the slowest phase-out of protection for any commodity under the agreement.[8]

The price advantage of US maize has four sources:

1. natural factors, notably better soils, more regular rainfall, and a killing frost that limits pest populations in the US corn belt;
2. farm subsidies that reduce the US market price;
3. the exclusion from market prices of environmental costs such as groundwater contamination, which is of greater importance in the USA, where agrochemical use is more intensive, than in Mexico; and
4. the failure of market prices to value the maintenance of genetic diversity by Mexican maize farmers.

NAFTA will not completely eliminate maize production in Mexico. Large-scale Mexican growers on the best soils, many of whom use US-style production techniques – including commercial hybrid varieties, irrigation, and intensive agrochemical applications – probably will be able to compete successfully. And very small-scale growers producing solely for their own household consumption might be less sensitive to the market price.[9]

NAFTA is likely to result in a substantial contraction of Mexico's maize acreage in the years ahead, however, as imported US maize displaces domestic production. Much of the abandoned maize land will be converted into cattle pastures, requiring far less labor. Estimates of the number of Mexican maize farmers who will be displaced by US imports vary widely. Relatively conservative estimates predict that hundreds of thousands of *campesinos* will migrate to Mexican cities (and perhaps to the USA) as a result. Upper-end predictions of the number of migrants run as high as 15 million people – one-sixth of the Mexican population.[10]

The extent of *campesino* displacement could be mitigated by government measures to support 'modernization' of maize production and diversification to other crops (de Janvry *et al.* 1995). In a similar vein, Levy and van Wijnbergen (1995) advocate a program of public investment in land improvements, notably irrigation, to offset losses to Mexican maize farmers. Such support would represent a marked departure from the policy trends of recent years, which have seen cutbacks in marketing, credit, and technical assistance services for small farmers. Even if such policies were forthcoming, however, they would not necessarily arrest the erosion of genetic diversity in maize; indeed, they could accelerate it.

In the face of this prospect, only limited comfort can be drawn from the fact that seed samples of many Mexican maize varieties are stored at CIMMYT and several gene banks around the world. It would be difficult to overstate the value of these *ex situ* (off-site) collections. But they do not provide a satisfactory substitute for on-the-ground, *in situ* genetic diversity for three reasons.

First, the gene banks are not completely secure. Accidents happen. So do wars. The seeds must be stored under controlled temperature and humidity conditions, and periodically regenerated by planting to harvest new seed. In the 1980s, the world's largest maize germplasm collection was at the Vavilov Institute in St. Petersburg; the second largest was in Belgrade (Plucknett *et al.* 1987: 120). Today the viability of the seeds in both collections is an open question. Even in relatively wealthy and stable countries such as the United States, plant breeders routinely lament the inadequate funding for seed collection maintenance from financially strapped governments. Irreplaceable material in gene banks has already been lost as a result of human error and mechanical failures. At CIMMYT, for example, maize collections from the 1940s were lost (Wade 1974: 1187); 'back-up copies' of Mexican maize at the US National Seed Storage Laboratory in Fort Collins, Colorado, were destroyed as well (Raeburn 1995: 62–3).

Second, many genetic attributes of crop varieties can be identified only by growing them in micro-habitats similar to those from which they originated. For example, the fact that a particular Mexican maize variety has a gene which enables it to withstand droughts at four-week intervals will not be apparent unless the plant is grown under those specific conditions. The alternative of expressing such genetic attributes in laboratory growth chambers is extremely costly.

Finally, even if it were possible to establish perfectly secure gene banks (which it is not), these could at best store only the existing stock of genetic diversity at any point in time. The ongoing process of evolution, which gave us this diversity and which continues to yield a flow of new varieties, cannot be stored in the bank; it can happen only in the field. Plant breeders can develop new crosses from the existing genetic stock, but they cannot replace the flow of new raw material from the evolutionary gardens.[11]

None of this implies that *ex situ* gene banks are unnecessary. On the contrary, the world needs more gene banks, better funding for them, and more investment in professional training for plant breeders whose knowledge is an essential complement to the gene banks (Wilkes 1992). Modern plant breeding has played a central role in the rapid growth in world food output in the past 50 years. Moreover, as recent experiences in Nicaragua and Cambodia have shown, *in situ* biodiversity is also vulnerable to losses – due to wars, among other causes – and in these cases *ex situ* collections provide crucial back-up copies (Plucknett *et al.* 1987: 94). But, while necessary, *ex situ* collections are not sufficient to sustain the genetic diversity on which long-term world food security ultimately rests. The gene banks are vital complements to *in situ* biodiversity, but not substitutes for it.

The competition between Mexican and US maize thus entails both positive and negative externalities. The positive externality – the conservation and evolution of crop genetic diversity – is generated south of the border. The negative externalities arising from intensive agrochemical use are concentrated north of the border, though they also characterize 'modern' Mexican maize farming. Under free trade, the Mexican *campesinos* who generate positive externalities sell at prices that fail to internalize the full social benefit of their production, while US producers sell at prices that fail to internalize the full social cost. The resulting double market failure not only undermines sustainable rural livelihoods in Mexico, but also jeopardizes the long-term sustainability of this key food crop worldwide.

POLICY IMPLICATIONS

With the increasing integration of world markets comes a corresponding need for international policy responses to market failures. Unilateral measures by individual governments can have only limited impacts on trade-driven market failures. To confront such problems as the erosion of crop genetic diversity and the displacement of renewable natural raw materials by pollution-intensive synthetic substitutes, multilateral initiatives are necessary.

Such initiatives could advance the goal of sustainable agriculture, with 'sustainability' understood to mean maintaining the production of food and fiber sufficient to meet the needs of current and future generations worldwide. By this definition, sustainable agriculture implies neither the world-wide hegemony of 'modern' agriculture nor a romantic return to 'traditional' agriculture. Instead the world needs both high-productivity, low-diversity 'modern' farming *and* low-productivity, high-diversity 'traditional' farming (and intermediate technologies which combine the two). Productivity is vital for world food security in the short run, and diversity is vital for world food security in the long run.

In the absence of corrective policies, the market rewards only short-run productivity as measured by price. One limitation of this myopic standard was noted by Schumpeter (1976: 83):

> A system – any system, economic or otherwise – that at *every* point in time fully utilizes its possibilities to the best advantage may yet in the long run be inferior to a system that does so at *no* point in time, because the latter's failure to do so may be a condition for the level or speed of long-run performance.

The role of crop genetic diversity in long-run agricultural performance illustrates Schumpeter's point.

In the discussions of trade and the environment at multilateral forums such as the United Nations Conference on Trade and Development and the World Trade Organization, it is often assumed that negative externalities are more prevalent in the South, while in the North, tougher regulations have led to a greater internalization of environmental costs.[12] The threat of 'environmental dumping' – exports at prices below the full cost of production, including the social costs of pollution – is therefore viewed primarily as a route by which Southern producers may win markets at the expense of their Northern competitors.

The examples discussed in this chapter illustrate the opposite possibility: international trade can result in the displacement of relatively clean and sustainable Southern production by environmentally more costly and less sustainable Northern production. Indeed, if one reflects on the history of international commerce since the Industrial Revolution, it is arguable that the main direction of environmental dumping has been from North to South.

Southern governments have been slow to call for policies that would help them to translate the comparative *environmental* advantages of their farmers into comparative *economic* advantages. In the case of jute, for example, the main response to the challenge from synthetics has been an effort to diversify into new end-uses for the natural fiber. Little serious attempt has been made to defend jute's position in its traditional end-use markets on the basis of its lower environmental costs. In the case of maize, the Mexican government is actually dismantling the quotas, tariffs, and price supports which provided some protection to Mexican farmers, reflecting both the government's embrace of neoliberal ideology and the declining political clout of the country's *campesinos*.

Yet the governments of the developing countries have an opportunity to move beyond a defensive posture in trade negotiations – in which they are cast as the international laggards in environmental protection – to a more positive stance as proponents of sustainable agriculture. They can draw support for this stance from the international environmental movement and, in particular, from citizens in the North who bear the environmental costs of pollution-intensive production. A genuine 'greening of world trade' could help to secure the livelihoods of some of the poorest people in the world today – the small farmers and agricultural laborers of developing countries – as well as the well-being of future generations worldwide.

NOTES

I wish to thank M. Asaduzzaman, Stephen Brush, Peter Dorman, Andrew Klemer, J. Mohan Rao, James Scott, and H. Garrison Wilkes for comments on earlier versions of this chapter. I also thank seminar participants at the University of California, Riverside, the University of Massachusetts, Amherst, Yale University, and the Third Biennial Meeting of the International Society for Ecological Economics for useful discussions. Research for this study was supported by a Faculty Research Grant from the University of Massachusetts, Amherst. I am grateful to Roohi Prem Baveja, Kevin Cahill, Nasrin Dalirazar, and Mariano Torras for research assistance.

1. Based on calculations by Maizels (1992: 189, 1995: 108), who reports that substitution reduced the developed market-economy countries' consumption of natural raw materials by 2.9 percent per year from 1963–5 to 1971–3, 0.9 percent per year from 1971–3 to 1978–80, and 1.2 percent per year from 1978–80 to 1984–6.

2. The nominal price of raw jute was $299/ton in 1972 (World Bank 1992: 12) and $277/ton in 1992–3 (IJO 1993: 4). The real price trend is here calculated using the US producer price index as a deflator.

3. Dixon and Mason (1994) summarize various damage cost estimates, ranging from $5.3– 50/ton of carbon in the decade 1991–2000 and rising to $6.8–120/ton in the following decade. Pearce *et al.* (1995: 68) report similar estimates.

4. This can be regarded as a lower-bound estimate insofar as (a) landfill costs are higher in more densely populated countries; (b) landfills are publicly subsidized; (c) landfills generate negative externalities; and/or (d) the improper disposal of PP is common, and this generates higher environmental costs than disposal in landfills.

5. Plant breeders rely heavily on selected 'elite' breeding lines for the production of new hybrids. The traditional 'landraces' from the farmers' fields provided the original genetic material in these lines, and landraces continue to be used as the main source for introducing greater diversity into them. For discussion, see Duvick (1984).

6. A 1994 survey of *ejido* maize producers in Mexico found that only 35 percent used herbicides, insecticides, or fungicides. For small farmers (cultivating less than 2 hectares), medium farmers (2–10 hectares), and large farmers (more than 10 hectares), the shares using any of these pesticides were 15 percent, 34 percent, and 51 percent, respectively (calculated from data reported by Secretaría de Reforma Agraria 1995: 5.17 and 5.19).

7. In 1994, citing concerns about human cancer risks and effects on aquatic organisms, the US Environmental Protection Agency (1994) launched a Special Review of atrazine and two closely related herbicides.

8. Mexican resistance to US corn imports was one of the most difficult issues in the negotiation of NAFTA's agriculture chapter. In return for the 15-year phase-out, Mexico agreed to allow the immediate duty-free import of up to 2 million mt of US corn per year (Thurston and Negrete 1992).

9. De Janvry *et al.* (1995) cite survey data which indicate that roughly half of *ejido* maize growers do not produce market surpluses, and conclude that neglect of this fact has caused other studies to overstate the labor displacement likely to result from NAFTA. Even among these growers, however, some households may shift to cheap imported corn to meet consumption needs, resulting in further contraction of maize acreage.

10. Estimates prepared for the World Bank indicate that in the first five years of NAFTA, between 145,000 and 300,000 farmers could abandon their land (DePalma 1993). José Luis Calva (1992: 35) of the National Autonomous University of Mexico predicted that total rural out-migration, including family members, could reach 15 million people. For other estimates, see Levy and Wijnbergen (1991), Robinson *et al.* (1991), and Harvey and Marblestone (1993).

11. For further discussion of the need and potential for *in situ* conservation of crop genetic resources, see Prescott-Allen and Prescott-Allen (1982), Altieri and Merrick (1987), and Brush (1992, 1995).

12. Some authors (for example, Grossman and Krueger 1995) find evidence of an 'environmental Kuznets curve,' whereby total pollution at first rises and then declines as per capita income grows. Chapter 5 offers evidence that changes in the distribution of power, rather than income alone, explain declines in pollution.

REFERENCES

Alam, A. (1993), 'Jute retting and environment,' in *Improved Retting and Extraction of Jute and Kenaf: Proceedings of Regional Workshop held at Research Institute for Tobacco and Fiber Crops, Malang, Indonesia, 1–6 February 1993*, Rome: Food and Agriculture Organisation of the United Nations; and Dhaka: International Jute Organisation, pp. 362–71.

Altieri, M.A. and Merrick, L.C. (1987), 'In situ conservation of crop genetic resources through maintenance of traditional farming systems,' *Economic Botany*, 41 (1): 86–96.

Boyce, J.K. (1995), 'Jute, polypropylene, and the environment: A study in international trade and market failure,' *Bangladesh Development Studies*, 13: 49–66.

Boyce, J.K. (1996), 'Ecological distribution, agricultural trade liberalization, and *in situ* genetic diversity,' *Journal of Income Distribution*, 6(2): 263–84.

Braungart, M., Engelfried, J., Hansen, K., Mulhall, D. and Neumann, A. (1992), 'Jute and polypropylene: Environmentally intelligent products? Comparative impact assessment,' Hamburg: Environmental Protection Encouragement Agency.

Brush, S. (1992), 'Farmers' rights and genetic conservation in traditional farming systems,' *World Development*, 20(11): 1617–30.

Brush, S. (1995), '*In situ* conservation of landraces in centers of crop diversity,' *Crop Science*, 35: 346–54.

Calva, J.L. (1992), *Probables Efectos de un Tratado de Libre Comercio en el Campo Mexicano*, Mexico City: Fontamara.

De Janvry, A., Sadoulet, E. and Gordillo de Anda, G. (1995), 'NAFTA and Mexico's maize producers,' *World Development*, 23(8): 1349–62.

DePalma, A. (1993), 'Mexicans fear for corn, imperiled by free trade,' *New York Times*, 12 July: A3.

Dixon, J.A. and Mason, J. (1994), 'Global warming: Measuring the costs,' World Bank, Environmentally Sustainable Development Vice Presidency, Dissemination Note no. 4, Washington, DC: World Bank.

Duvick, D.N. (1984), 'Genetic diversity in major farm crops on the farm and in reserve,' *Economic Botany*, 38(2): 161–78.

Food and Agriculture Organization (FAO) (1994), *Trade Yearbook 1993*, Rome: FAO.

Grossman, G.M. and Krueger, A.B. (1995), 'Economic growth and the environment,' *Quarterly Journal of Economics*, 110: 353–77.

Harvey, N. and Marblestone, J. (1993), 'Emptying the fields? NAFTA and Mexican agriculture,' *Brown Foreign Affairs Journal*, 6(1): 2–10.

Hye, S.A. (1993), 'Review on labour and employment,' in M. Asaduzzaman and K. Westergaard (eds), *Growth and Development in Rural Bangladesh: A Critical Review*, Dhaka: University Press: 261–406.

International Jute Organisation (IJO) (1993), 'Review of jute situation and policies affecting jute production and trade', International Jute Council 20th Session. 3–5 November 1993, Dhaka, Bangladesh.

Johnson, E. (1990), 'Polypropylene: action plan,' *Chemical Engineering*, May: 30–7.

Levy, S. and van Wijnbergen, S. (1991), 'El maíz y el acuerdo de libre comercio entre México y los Estados Unidos,' *El Trimestre Económico*, 58(4): 823–62.

Levy, S. and van Wijnbergen, S. (1995), 'Transition problems in economic reform:

Agriculture in the North American Free Trade Agreement,' *American Economic Review*, 85(4): 738–54.

Maizels, A. (1992), *Commodities in Crisis: The Commodity Crisis of the 1980s and the Political Economy of International Commodity Prices*, Oxford: Clarendon Press.

Maizels, A. (1995), 'The functioning of international markets for primary commodities: Key policy issues for developing countries,' in United Nations Conference on Trade and Development (UNCTAD), *International Monetary and Financial Issues for the 1990s: Research Papers for the Group of Twenty-Four*, Volume V, New York and Geneva: United Nations.

Pearce, D.W., Cline, W.R., Achanta, A.N., Fankhauser, S., Pachauri, R.K., Tol, R.S.J. and Vellinga, P. (1995), 'The social costs of climate change: Greenhouse damage and the benefits of control,' draft, April.

Plucknett, D.L., Smith, N.J.H., Williams, J.T. and Anishetty, N.M. (1987), *Gene Banks and the World's Food*, Princeton, NJ: Princeton University Press.

Prescott-Allen, R. and Prescott-Allen, C. (1982), 'The case for *in situ* conservation of crop genetic resources,' *Nature and Resources*, 18(1): 15–20.

Raeburn, P. (1995), *The Last Harvest: The Genetic Gamble that Threatens to Destroy American Agriculture*, New York: Simon & Schuster.

Robinson, S., Burfisher, M.E., Hinojosa-Ojeda, R. and Thierfelder, K.E. (1991), 'Agricultural policies and migration in a US–Mexico Free Trade Area: A computable general equilibrium analysis,' Working Paper no. 617, Berkeley, CA: University of California, Department of Agricultural and Resource Economics.

Schumpeter, J. (1976), *Capitalism, Socialism and Democracy*, 5th edn., London: George Allen & Unwin.

Scott, D.C. (1992), 'Trade deal with the United States puts many Mexican farmers at risk', *Christian Science Monitor*, 4 November: 10.

Secretaría de Reforma Agraria (1995), 'El sector ejidal en la agricultura Mexicana: Impacto de las reformas,' mimeo.

Tellus Institute (1992), *Tellus Institute Packaging Study*, Boston, MA: Tellus Institute and Council of State Governments.

Thigpen, M.E., Marongiu, P. and Lasker, S.R. (1987), 'World demand prospects for jute,' World Bank Staff Commodity Working Paper no. 16, Washington, DC: World Bank.

Thurston, C.W. and Negrete, I. (1992), 'Mexico yields on corn quota: Farm accord near,' *Journal of Commerce*, 15 July: 1A.

United Nations (1993), *Industrial Statistics Yearbook 1991, Volume II: Commodity Production Statistics 1982–1991*, New York: United Nations.

United States Environmental Protection Agency (EPA) (1990), *National Pesticide Survey: Atrazine*, Washington, DC: EPA, Office of Water and Office of Pesticides and Toxic Substances.

United States Environmental Protection Agency (EPA) (1994), 'EPA begins special review of triazine pesticides,' *EPA Environmental News*, Release 279, 10 November.

Vavilov, N.I. (1992), *Origin and Geography of Cultivated Plants*, Cambridge: Cambridge University Press.

Wade, N. (1974), 'Green Revolution (II): Problems of adapting a western technology,' *Science*, 186 (27 December): 1186–92.

Walsh, J. (1981), 'Genetic vulnerability down on the farm,' *Science*, 214 (9 October): 161–4.

Wilkes, H.G. (1992), *Strategies for Sustaining Crop Germplasm Preservation, Enhancement, and Use*, Washington, DC: Consultative Group for International Agricultural Research, Issues in Agriculture no. 5, October.

World Bank (1992), *Bangladesh: Restructuring Options for the Jute Manufacturing Industry*, Report no. 10052-BD, Washington, DC: World Bank.

8.   A squandered inheritance

INTRODUCTION

The trees in a forest, like the crops in a field, are products of the soil. However, they differ not only in botanical respects, such as the longer growing period, but also in two important institutional respects. First, unlike crop lands, forests are often in the public domain, posing open-access problems. Second, deforestation, a widespread but not inevitable consequence of timber extraction, gives rise to distinctive external costs, including soil erosion, watershed and climate modifications, and losses of biological diversity, which are not taken into account by the timber extractor. The two are interlinked: insecure and contested rights of access to public resources promote a 'cut-and-run' ethos in forest management, and the severity of negative externalities increases as a result.

This chapter examines the dynamics of deforestation in the Philippines during the rule of President Ferdinand Marcos (1966–1986). During the Marcos era, Philippine export earnings from forestry at times surpassed those from either of the country's leading export crops, coconut and sugarcane. As in export agriculture, the distribution of gains and losses reflected and reinforced profound inequalities of wealth and power. A small number of powerful individuals appropriated the benefits of public resources, while imposing the costs of negative externalities on others, including future generations of Filipinos.

Nominally, 90 percent of the Philippines' 18.7 million hectares (ha) of uplands, including more than 11 million ha officially classified as timberlands, is publicly owned (Cornista 1985: 1). In practice, however, fewer than 200 individuals controlled a large fraction of the country's forests during the Marcos era. A senior government official summarized their degree of control shortly after the overthrow of the Marcos regime: 'Some five million hectares are owned by 114 individuals.'[1] Forest lands were not 'owned' *de jure*, but rather were leased from the government by logging concessionaires. In practice, however, the *de facto* rights of the loggers were constrained more by political uncertainty than by effective social controls over land use.[2]

Prior to Marcos's declaration of martial law in 1972, logging leases were granted for periods of 1–10 years. In some cases, logging companies placed influential politicians on their boards of directors so as to obtain and renew leases. In other cases, politicians obtained the licenses themselves, and then rented them to logging firms. Given political uncertainties, most firms 'had no assurance that their lease would be renewed for another year, let alone that they would still be in the logging business many years hence' (Porter and Ganapin 1988: 26).

In the 1970s, timber leases were extended to a 25-year term, but this was still too short to provide an incentive for sustainable yield management or forest replanting. The 25-year leases could, in theory, be renewed, but few logging companies were sanguine enough to plan on the basis of a 50-year time horizon. Hence in the Philippines, as in many other countries, concession holders preferred 'to take their quotas as quickly as possible rather than establish long-term operations in a climate of political and economic uncertainty' (Caufield 1985a: 99). Logging firms acted as if their first cut was their last, initiating the process of deforestation.

THE COSTS OF DEFORESTATION

At the turn of the century, forests covered more than 20 million of the Philippines' 30 million hectares (ha). Since then the country has witnessed some of the most rapid deforestation in the world. In 1981 the Food and Agriculture Organization of the United Nations estimated that, of the remaining 9.5 million ha officially classified as 'closed forest,' only 3 million ha were undisturbed, and 2 million ha had been so severely degraded as to be incapable of regeneration (cited by Anderson 1987: 250). Reviewing a variety of estimates, Revilla (1984: 7–10) concluded that, as of 1983, 'forested forest lands' in the Philippines totaled 7.8 to 8.3 million ha, of which only 2.0–2.5 million ha represented old-growth forests. The US Agency for International Development (1985: 21) estimated the rate of net deforestation in the 1980s at 225,000 ha/year – an annual cut of 300,000 ha of mature stands as against annual reforestation of 75,000 ha – and predicted that the country's primary forests would 'virtually disappear' in the next 25 years.[3]

The Philippines led its Southeast Asian neighbors in a regional plunge into export logging and deforestation, beginning with an 'intensive marketing effort' for Philippine hardwoods in the early years of US colonial rule (Laarman 1988: 155). Tropical hardwood log exports from the 'big three' supplier countries – the Philippines, Malaysia, and Indonesia – grew at an 'astonishing pace' after World War Two, accelerating to 15 percent per year in the 1965–70 period (Takeuchi 1974: 4). The Philippines remained the region's biggest exporter until being overtaken by Malaysia and Indonesia in the early 1970s (FAO 1977: 304).

Southeast Asia in turn led the world in exports of tropical wood. In the decade after World War Two, technological improvements led to a sharp decline in production costs for plywood and veneer made from lauan ('Philippine mahogany'), opening large new wood product markets (Laarman 1988: 151). The big three Southeast Asian exporters together accounted for three-quarters of all log exports from the Third World in the early 1970s (Takeuchi 1974: 5). As late as 1980, the Asia-Pacific region as a whole accounted for more than 80 percent of Third World exports of logs and processed wood. But with the depletion of Southeast Asia's forests, the logging industry is rapidly shifting to Latin America and Africa, and the Asia-Pacific share was forecast to fall to 10 percent by the year 2000 (Scott 1989: 38).

The social costs that deforestation has imposed on present and future generations of Filipinos include: (a) the loss of future income opportunities in the forestry sector; (b) the climatic impacts of watershed modification; and (c) the loss of biological diversity and depletion of genetic resources.

Loss of Future Income Opportunities

In effect, the forests of Southeast Asia have been treated as free goods. As Guppy (1984: 954) remarks, 'the price of tropical trees *in the forest* is negligible' (emphasis in original). Log supply prices have been based almost entirely on the costs of resource extraction, that is, felling and transportation, without including the cost of reproduction.

On the demand side of the tropical hardwood market, the most explosive growth in the postwar period occurred in Japan, whose share of world consumption grew from 4 percent in 1950 to roughly 50 percent in the 1980s (Laarman 1988: 160). Japan has been the single largest market for Philippine forestry exports.[4] Evidently the 'social discount rate' applied to Philippine forests has been rather different from that applied to Japan's own extensive domestic forest reserves. In the Philippines it has been quite high – the potential benefits of conserving forests for future generations have counted for little – while in Japan it has been much lower. According to one forestry expert, 'Japan has a very clear strategy: to protect its forests for as long as possible, although it means overexploitation of Southeast Asia and the Pacific region.'[5] The Organization for Economic Cooperation and Development (1991: 37) estimates that in the early 1980s Japan's domestic timber harvest extracted only 53 percent of the annual growth in its stock of trees. In other words, while the forest resources of Southeast Asia are being rapidly depleted, those of Japan are being augmented.

Tropical forests are in the intermediate area between renewable and non-renewable resources. Using techniques of 'sustainable yield management,' in which only fully mature trees are cut and damage to adjacent trees is minimized, it is possible to extract a stable harvest of mature hardwoods every three to five decades. Worldwide, less than 1 percent of tropical forests are currently managed in this way (Scott 1989: 35). If less-careful (and, in the short run, less-costly) logging techniques are employed, it is possible to plant new trees, either some of the original long-maturing hardwoods or faster-growing species, preserving tree cover and soil if not the diversity of the original ecosystem.

Philippine forestry practices, however, have pushed the country's forests towards the non-renewable pole of the resource continuum. The typical pattern begins with intensive logging, in which immediately profitable trees are extracted with no concern for the surrounding vegetation. The Asian Development Bank (1987: 117) estimates that 'extracted volume may represent only 20 to 40 percent of the total volume by which the growing stock is reduced in a logging operation,' the remainder being attributable to the opening of roads and skid trails, damages to adjacent trees, and discarded residues.[6]

The roads built by the logging industry not only carry the logs out, but also carry settlers in. Logged-over areas are slashed and burnt to clear the land for agricultural use. Initially, rice, corn, and other annual crops are grown. But the fertility of the upland soils rapidly diminishes once the forest cover is removed, due to soil erosion, the loss of organic matter, and the leaching of nutrients. Within as little as four years, the land becomes unable to support annual cropping, and the settlers either move to newly cleared lands or switch to less demanding tree crops. The abandoned land is often overgrown by coarse grasses. This in turn attracts cattle ranchers, who periodically burn the grass to provide tender young shoots for grazing. The fires further reduce the humus content of the soil and kill any tree seedlings that might have sprouted. Finally the land becomes too poor even for cattle.[7]

When mistreated in this fashion, the tropical rainforest becomes a non-renewable resource. In the Philippines, the constraint of non-renewability began to bind in the 1970s. After more than doubling in the 1960s, exports of logs and lumber fell from 4 billion board feet in 1970 to less than 1 billion in 1985. At the same time, the terms of trade for forestry exports declined sharply, reflecting increasing supplies from other Third World countries, often accompanied by similar deforestation. As a result, by 1985 the purchasing power of total Philippine earnings from exports of logs and lumber was less than a quarter of its 1962 level, and only 13 percent of the 1970 peak (Boyce 1993: 229).

Herein lies the first social cost of the Philippine forestry 'development' strategy: the contraction of current and future income opportunities in the forestry sector itself. The full magnitude of this cost will be multiplied in coming decades when, as a result of worldwide deforestation, the prices of tropical hardwoods rise 'until eventually they reach the cost of replacement'

(Guppy 1984: 953).[8] A cruel irony is that by the time world prices rise to a sustainable-yield level, the Philippines is likely to have become a net importer of wood, its own resources having been depleted to the point at which they no longer suffice to meet domestic needs.[9]

Watershed Modification and Climatic Effects

Hydrological and climatic changes caused by deforestation give rise to a second set of social costs. In the Philippines, as in many countries, the forest acts as a sponge, absorbing water in the rainy season and gradually releasing it in the dry season. The forest vegetation and soil catch and hold the rainfall, returning about 60 percent of it to the atmosphere via evaporation and plant transpiration, and letting about 40 percent drain into rivers. The beneficial results include a smoothing of the time distribution of water discharge, the minimization of soil erosion, and the enhancement of runoff water quality (David 1984: 5, 10).

Deforestation destroys this 'sponge effect.' In the rainy months, rapid runoff leads to floods downstream. Soil erosion leads to the siltation of waterways and reservoirs, exacerbating floods and reducing water storage capacities. And in the dry months, reduced river flow leads to water shortage and drought.

Flying over the deforested uplands of the Philippines, one can see whole mountainsides being washed away. In the watershed of the Agno River in central Luzon, for example, by the mid-1970s all of the topsoil and half of the subsoil had been eroded from nearly 60,000 ha, and 75 percent of the topsoil had been lost from another 125,000 ha; downstream, meanwhile, the river was so heavily silted that in some places it flowed higher than the surrounding rice fields, so that a break in its banks could cause severe floods (Porter and Ganapin 1988: 24). A study of river sediment loads in 1978 revealed soil losses of 45 metric tons per hectare (mt/ha) per year. In the still-forested Marbel basin of Mindanao, by contrast, the sediment yield was less than one mt/ha/year.[10]

Massive siltation has sharply reduced the useful life span of the Ambuklao Dam on the Agno River, which was built for hydroelectric power generation in the 1950s with US Export–Import Bank finance. At the time of its construction, Ambuklao was the second-highest earth and rock fill dam in the world, and it created the largest man-made lake in the Philippines (Zablan 1961: 2). In its cost-benefit analysis, Ambuklao was projected to operate for 75 years, but siltation cut this in half.[11] Similarly, the World Bank reports that the Magat reservoir in Cagayan, intended to supply water to the largest irrigation system in the country, has had its probable life span cut by siltation from 100 years at the project appraisal in the 1970s to as little as 25 years.[12]

Floods have also imposed large social costs. In the typhoon belt from northern Luzon to southern Samar, flooding has increased greatly as a result of watershed degradation, according to a 1982 FAO study.[13] In the Cagayan Valley, for example, entire villages have 'washed into the rivers during some typhoons, a catastrophe people in the valley had never witnessed before the loggers came to the mountains' (Porter and Ganapin 1988: 25). In Zambales province in central Luzon, rainy-season floods regularly wash out highways and bridges, while during the dry season, owing to the loss of the forest sponge, droughts have curtailed vegetable gardening and fishing (*ibid.*). In Mindanao, south of the typhoon belt, denuded forests have also led to cata-strophic floods. Floods in Northern Mindanao in 1981, for example, killed 283 people, injured 14,000, and left tens of thousands homeless (Tadem *et al.* 1984: 4).

In addition to these severe local externalities, tropical deforestation con-tributes to worldwide climatic change by altering the global carbon cycle. Tropical forests contain about 20 percent of the world's terrestrial carbon, roughly half in the living forest and half in the soil. Much of this is released as carbon dioxide when the forest is destroyed (Guppy 1984: 931). The accumulation of carbon dioxide and other gases in the atmosphere traps more heat near the earth's surface, and a number of scientists predict that the resulting global 'greenhouse effect' will cause temperatures to rise in coming decades, triggering far-reaching disruptions in weather patterns and world agriculture. Potential consequences in the Philippines include changes in rainfall patterns and the submergence of low-lying coastal areas, including parts of metropolitan Manila, by rising sea levels caused by the melting of the polar ice caps. The Philippines bears only a minor share of responsibility for the global greenhouse effect, however, since the primary cause of rising atmospheric carbon dioxide levels has been fossil fuel combustion in the industrialized countries.[14] Like most developing countries, the Philippines is likely to be mainly on the receiving end of the greenhouse effect, its share of the adverse impacts outweighing its contribution to the problem.

Loss of Biological Diversity

Although tropical rainforests cover only a small fraction of the earth's sur-face, they are home to roughly half of the world's plant and animal species. Rainforests in general support extraordinarily diverse plant and animal populations, and those of Southeast Asia exceed all others in this respect. Dr T.C. Whitmore, a leading authority on the subject, concludes: 'The tropical rain forests of the Far East include the most complex and species-rich ecosys-tems which have ever existed on this planet.'[15] For example, the slopes of a single volcano in Luzon's Laguna and Batangas provinces, Mt Makiling, contain as many woody plant species as the entire United States (Caufield 1985b: 60). Many rainforest species remain unknown to scientists. About half a million species have been identified, but Raven (1987: 11) estimates that 'there are at least 3 million, and perhaps ten times that many, yet to be discovered.'

Tropical deforestation currently results in the extinction of an estimated 10,000 plant and animal species each year (Scott 1989: 34). Caufield (1985a: 59) reports that, 'Fewer than one percent of tropical-forest species have been examined for their possible use to mankind – that is, screened for chemical compounds.'

Although the economic value of rainforest species is unknown, and indeed unknowable given uncertainty as to future human needs, a few examples will give an indication of the stakes. In searching for a rice plant gene for resistance to grassy-stunt virus, scientists at the International Rice Research Institute screened thousands of varieties. They found only one such gene, in two seeds of a wild rice variety which had been collected in central India. When scientists returned to the source area, they were unable to find any more. As a result, Caufield (*ibid.*) reports, 'every modern rice plant has a gene derived from one of those two original seeds.' In addition to agriculture, biological resources have important medical uses. One-quarter of all pharmaceuticals originate from plants and animals of tropical forests (World Bank 1989: 67). The US National Cancer Institute has identified 3000 plants with anti-cancer properties, 70 percent of which are rainforest species (Caufield 1985a: 60).

Since the potential benefits extend to all of humankind, the preservation of biological diversity is a textbook example of a public good.[16] The loss of species through deforestation hence arises from the combined effect of three disjunctures between individual and social rationality: (a) the myopia, or excessively high discount rates, of individuals; (b) the externality problem that the costs of species losses are social while the benefits of forest destruction are private; and (c) the 'free rider' problem that *even if* costs of biodiversity loss exceeded benefits for the individual, a 'rational' maximizer of self-interest would continue to cut the forest to minimize his or her personal loss, on the assumption that others would cut if s/he did not.[17]

Various proposals have been put forward to conserve the genetic resources of tropical rainforests. These range from 'living gene banks' in the form of parks and reserves to the collection and preservation of samples in botanical gardens, seed banks, and tissue culture centers (Raven 1987: 16). In practice, such efforts have been quite limited, and even if they were much better developed, they would provide only an imperfect substitute for natural environments for at least two reasons. First, centralized conservation means putting one's eggs in a few baskets, with the attendant risks of losses due to man-made or natural disasters. Second, for both scientific and aesthetic purposes (including tourism), natural environments are more than the sum of their component species.

Together, the social costs of Philippine deforestation include the loss of future forestry income, the degradation of watersheds, climatic disruptions, and the reduction of biological diversity. While the benefits of deforestation have accrued to a small number of people, notably the captains of the logging industry, the costs have been distributed widely. Some of these costs affect people outside the Philippines, but the heaviest ones have been imposed on present and future generations of Filipinos.

PUBLIC RESOURCES AND PRIVATE INTERESTS

Most of the Philippines' forests are in the public domain, and over the years successive governments have promulgated forestry rules and regulations which aim, at least in theory, to safeguard the public interest. The inefficacy of these attempts reflects not only a lack of resources for enforcement, but also the distribution of wealth and power in Philippine society.

The allocation of logging licenses in the Philippines has long been a vehicle for political patronage. During martial law, there were reportedly 'two ways to obtain a timber concession: either by knowing the President, or knowing someone in the Wood Industries Development Board' (Hurst 1990: 187). Lucrative concessions were 'gobbled up by cronies of Marcos's' (Porter and Ganapin 1988: 27). Defense Minister Juan Ponce Enrile controlled logging companies with leases totaling hundreds of thousands of hectares. Another close Marcos associate, Herminio Disini, obtained nearly 200,000 ha in timber concessions in northern Luzon, including tribal lands of the Tinggian cultural minority.[18]

Foreign firms have long been involved in Philippine timber extraction. The rapid exploitation of the country's forests began early in the twentieth century, as US firms entered in partnership with logging companies formed by the landowning elite.[19] Major transnational companies in the Philippine timber industry in the 1970s and 1980s included Georgia-Pacific, Boise-Cascade, International Paper, Weyerhaeuser, and Mitsubishi.[20]

Forest management provisions in the logging licenses – such as selective cutting and reforestation requirements – are often ignored by licensees. Much unlicensed logging also occurs, often with *de facto* official protection. For example, in an area of northern Luzon in which logging is nominally banned, trucks loaded with logs reportedly pay 'tolls' as they pass military checkpoints in leaving the forest (Mackenzie 1988: 43). On the Agusan River in northeastern Mindanao, Tadem *et al.* (1984: 156) found numerous unauthorized military checkpoints involved in extortion, sardonically called by loggers the 'fourteen stations of the cross.' A retired forestry official remarked, 'There is reason to believe that illegal logging will not prosper if there is no backing from some law enforcers and the military' (Reyes 1984: 49).

Some loggers deploy their own private armies. The main logging baron in Palawan, for example, 'routinely operates outside the nominal boundaries of the Timber Concession Agreements granted by the central government,' but objections are muted by the fact that he 'maintains considerable numbers of private security guards and has an intemperate reputation' (Clad and Vitug 1988: 50). Similar circumstances are expressed in the rhetorical question of a Mindanao official: 'What would you do as a forestry officer manning an isolated road block if a dozen armed men pushed the barrels of their rifles down your nose and politely requested you to let their log-laden trucks through?'[21] The total volume of illegal logging in the Philippines is unknown, but the World Bank (1989: 11) states that its addition to the licensed timber cut might double the total estimated volume of annual extraction.

Some logging also takes a quasi-legal form. For example, logging firms owned by friends of President Marcos were allowed to cut timber on lands legally leased to others, under the pretext of clearing the forest for Ministry of Agrarian Reform resettlement projects (Porter and Ganapin 1988: 27).

When the Philippine government imposed a quota on log exports in the late 1970s, in an attempt to slow deforestation and encourage domestic wood processing industries, the law was flouted by smugglers. Comparisons of trade data reveal massive under-reporting of log exports: in 1980, for example, Japan reported 1.1 billion cubic meters of hardwood log imports from the Philippines, while Philippine government data on exports to Japan recorded less than half that amount.[22] Ernesto Maceda, who became Minister of Natural Resources after the February 1986 revolution, estimated that between 1974 and 1980, US $960 million worth of timber was smuggled out of the country by friends and associates of President Marcos (Crewdson 1986: 21).

The level of government license fees – in effect, the rent paid by private loggers for the appropriation of public resources – similarly reveals the weakness of public *vis-à-vis* private interests. The pattern was established in the early years of US colonial rule, when logging concessions were dispensed on 'ruinously favorable terms.'[23] Including export tax receipts as well as license fees, total Philippine government revenue from the forestry sector from 1979 to 1982 amounted to $170 million, only 11.4 percent of the $1.5 billion potential rent.[24] Repetto (1988: 15) notes that annual government revenues 'have not covered even the administrative and infrastructure costs incurred for timber harvesting.'

The Bureau of Forestry Development (BFD), the government agency charged with the implementation of forest policies, was dubbed the 'Bureau of Forest Destruction' by critics because of 'its readiness to protect loggers for a price' (Porter and Ganapin 1988: 28). The Assistant Director of the BFD frankly assessed the agency's reputation in 1982: 'For the past many years, government foresters have time and again been accused of catering mostly to the whims and fancies of moneyed politicians and cunning timber and other forest product exploiters.'[25]

After the downfall of the Marcos regime, the BFD sought to improve its image by aiming to 'democratize the disposition of public lands' (Alvarez 1987: 2). This is easier said than done, however. The dominant logger in Palawan, for example, reportedly maintained his control of 168,000 ha of logging concessions simply by switching political allegiance after February 1986.[26]

International actors have played key roles in Philippine forestry. Foreign demand has provided the main impetus for the logging industry; foreign firms have directly engaged in logging; and international agencies have influenced government policy. As early as 1962, a World Bank report described the country's forestry policies as 'irresponsible' and 'suicidal':

> Earnings from forestry and forest products have skyrocketed since World War II, though at a cost which is beginning to resemble a bargain sale of the Filipino birthright. ... The combined effects of *kaingin* farming and 'legal' slaughter of the forest include widespread erosion and a reported deterioration in climatic conditions.   (World Bank 1962: 16, 18.)

This warning went unheeded not only by the Philippine government but by the Bank itself. A decade later, at the height of the country's forestry export boom, the World Bank's primary concern was 'efficiency,' writ small:

> The extensive forest resources of the Philippines appear to offer good prospects for increasing export earnings during the 1970s, but they are not managed well. Output of trees under license falls short of the allowable cut level ... Policies which encourage more efficient use of the forests and low-cost production in order to compete with other log exporters to Japan should be established.   (World Bank 1973: I.20)

The World Bank offered more than words of encouragement for continued forest exploitation.[27] As part of its Smallholder [*sic*] Tree Farming and Forestry Project, for example, the Bank funded a tree plantation on ancestral lands of the Tinggian minority to supply a pulp mill of Cellophil, a corporation established by Marcos associate Herminio Disini.[28] The same firm received $113.5 million in loans from European commercial banks, repayment of which was guaranteed by the government's Development Bank of the Philippines (Kramer 1978: 18).

UPLAND AGRICULTURE: BLAMING THE VICTIM

Once opened up by the loggers, many forest areas have been cleared for agricultural use. The usual technique is slash-and-burn cultivation, known as *kaingin* in the Philippines, an imprecise term often used to encompass the ecologically sustainable techniques of traditional forest dwellers, as well as the ecologically non-sustainable techniques of migrants from the lowlands.[29]

In recent decades the upland population appears to have grown at roughly the same rate as the country's population as a whole.[30] Some regions, such as Southern and Central Mindanao, witnessed considerable migration into upland areas. In other regions, such as the Visayas, the upland population grew more slowly than the national average, implying net out-migration (Cruz *et al.* 1986).

The allocation of agricultural land-use rights in upland areas, like the allocation of logging rights, has been shaped by the distribution of power. In the Philippines, as elsewhere, the new property rights established in the land frontier bear the indelible imprint of the colonists' social order. As elsewhere, too, the newcomers have often disregarded the traditional rights of the tribal 'cultural minorities' who have inhabited the uplands for many generations.[31]

The disregard of traditional rights can be traced as far back as Magellan's annexation of the Philippines on behalf of the Spanish royal family in 1521: 'The legal effect of Magellan's gesture was to convert all of the indigenous forest occupants of the still unexplored archipelago into squatters.'[32] This usurpation continued under US colonial rule, notwithstanding a 1909 US Supreme Court decision recognizing 'native titles.'[33]

Although they occupy what is nominally public land, many upland settlers pay rent to private 'landlords.' Little documentation of the origins, extent, and nature of these *de facto* tenancy relationships is available. Porter and Ganapin (1988: 29) report that 'an unknown number' of upland cultivators 'are part of a well-organized occupation of forest land being carried out by wealthier individuals hoping to lay claim to the land by paying taxes on it.' These 'taxes' are paid to local officials in an attempt to purchase their support. Cornista (1985: 2–3) reports that these 'non-cultivating claimants' are 'generally absentees,' and that they act as 'virtual landowners,' usually extracting share rents from their tenants.

In some instances, local judicial systems have been mobilized in support of these claims. For example, Borlagdan (1990: 273) mentions a case in Cebu in which an absentee claimant filed a legal complaint against a settler who had not surrendered a share of his harvests:

Because the landlord had no legal title to the land, he filed a complaint for breach
of contract over the sharing agreement, a personal contract between the tenant and
the claimant. The case was dismissed after the tenant apologized to the claimant
and swore to resume compliance with the sharing agreement.

In those areas of settlement in which legal titles are issued, Lopez (1987:
235) remarks that 'landed elites, with their strong political connections, wealth
and access to legal expertise, can more readily obtain titles than settlers or
cultural minorities,' and adds that 'even settlers enjoy a comparative advantage over indigenous groups.'

Official Philippine government policy towards agricultural settlement in
public-domain forest areas traditionally has been one of repression. The
Bureau of Forestry Development (BFD) 'long sought to eradicate *kaingin*-
making and forest occupancy, declaring them illegal and in fact prosecuting
those that have been caught' (Aguilar 1982: 2). Local populations, who bear
many of the heaviest social costs of deforestation, were seen as part of the
problem, rather than as part of the solution.

In the mid-1970s, the Philippine government moved towards 'social forestry' policies, which accept the reality of upland settlement and seek to
channel settler activities in what the government defines as socially desirable
directions. The revised Forestry Code, promulgated as Presidential Decree
No. 705 in 1975, stated:

> *Kaingineros*, squatters, cultural minorities and other occupants who entered into
> forest lands before the effectivity of this Code, without permits or authority, shall
> not be prosecuted: *provided*, that they do not increase their clearings; *provided,
> further*, that they undertake within two (2) months from notice thereof, the activi-
> ties *which will be imposed upon them by the Bureau* in accordance with a
> management plan calculated to conserve and protect forest resources.[34]   (Final
> emphasis added.)

The top-down approach of the new government policy is evident in the
language of the decree.

The social forestry policies included two long-term land tenure instruments: the Certificate of Stewardship Contract issued to individuals and the
Community Forest Lease issued to associations of individuals who will use
the land communally. Both extend for 25 years and are renewable thereafter,
with provisions for transfer to the next-of-kin. The programs encountered
resistance, however, from three sources: first, the cultivators themselves,
many of whom 'believe that it is simply a means of getting them to plant trees
and that BFD will reclaim the land once the trees have been grown'; second,
the elite non-cultivating claimants, who view the programs as a threat to their
efforts to appropriate the land; and third, local officials, who 'tend to side
with the claimants because they get revenues from the taxes paid on the

land.'[35] As of 1986, the BFD had issued stewardship certificates covering only 162,000 ha, and community forest leases covering only 16,000 ha, to a total of 65,000 households (Alvarez 1987: 5). The vast majority of upland cultivators thus continued to lack secure tenure.[36]

Loggers and government officials often identify the *kaingineros* as the principal culprits in Philippine deforestation. A 1980 government study, for example, attributed 55 percent of annual forest cover losses to *kaingineros*, 40 percent to legal logging and forest fires, and less than 5 percent to illegal logging (McCue 1982). Officials of a lumber company with a 95,000 ha forest concession in Mindanao similarly complain of 'the unstoppable entry and destruction caused by hordes of settlers and forest residents.'[37]

Although upland farmers often do contribute to deforestation, it is misleading to cast them as the main villains. Since clearing for cultivation typically follows the logging of the land, and grazing, in turn, often follows cultivation, one cannot neatly assign percentage shares of responsibility for deforestation to the different parties. Moreover, what distinguishes upland farmers from other agents of deforestation – loggers, government officials, absentee landlords, and international firms and institutions – is that the upland farmers themselves are among the principal *victims* of the deforestation process. Not coincidentally, they are also the poorest of these parties.

Some observers consider population pressure to be 'the underlying factor' behind Philippine deforestation.[38] This analysis in effect blames the victims twice: first for what they do, and then for why they do it. As Frederick Engels observed more than a century ago, 'the pressure of population is not upon the means of subsistence but upon the means of *employment*.'[39] The land hunger which drives impoverished cultivators to clear the forests is an outcome of the concentrated ownership of farmlands elsewhere in the country and of the absence of sufficient non-agricultural employment opportunities.[40]

On a visit to Bataan province in January 1989, I spoke with some cultivators who had occupied and cleared forest land belonging to a nearby paper mill. After slashing and burning the vegetation on the steep hillsides, they had planted bananas, papayas, and cassava. A recent typhoon had destroyed the flowers which would have produced their first fruit crop. For the past year they had subsisted almost entirely on boiled cassava root, the only food they could offer to a visitor. The cultivators had been previously working as agricultural laborers in Bataan, having migrated from the Visayas some 15 years earlier. Their last employer had been a landlord and trader, one of the richest men in the province, who had paid them poorly and often not on time. Although they were now suffering extreme deprivation in the hills, they assured me that they were in fact better off than they had been as laborers. 'Population pressure' in the Philippine uplands can be understood only within this political and economic context.[41]

In an impassioned 1988 pastoral letter, the Catholic Bishops Conference of the Philippines protested the despoliation of the country's environment: 'Our forests are almost gone, our rivers are almost empty,' the bishops wrote. 'During the monsoon rains, flash-floods destroy everything in their path.' Blaming 'the relentless drive of our plunder economy,' the bishops posed the crucial question: 'Who has benefited most, and who has borne the real costs?'[42]

This question is important not only for a diagnosis of the problem, but also for its implications as to the political impetus for change. The clash between private and public interests in Philippine forestry is at the same time a clash between rich and poor. Those who bear the heaviest costs of deforestation have the greatest motivation to change the country's forestry policies. First and foremost, this means the rural poor.

For example, in 1987 a non-governmental organization successfully blocked logging on ancestral lands of the Mangyan cultural minority in Mindoro.[43] In the battle over the fate of the country's largest remaining virgin forest on the island of Palawan, the national environmental organization Haribon has attempted to forge links with diverse local residents, including former workers for the island's dominant logging firm.[44] Local communities often need national and even international support to thwart powerful logging interests, but their active engagement is likely to be the most basic precondition for the emergence of an alternative forestry policy.

CONCLUSIONS

Philippine forestry in the Marcos era provides a case study in the political economy of environmental degradation.[45] A natural inheritance has been squandered, as future income opportunities are sacrificed for short-term gains. At the same time, the social costs of soil erosion, floods, droughts, and loss of biological diversity have been imposed on current and future generations.

The neoclassical economist diagnoses these symptoms as a case of 'market failure': the pursuit of individual self-interest does not generate a socially desirable outcome, due to myopia and externalities. The political economist, however, recognizes a further source of the malady: the distribution of power. The ability to seize natural resources for personal benefit and to impose social costs on others is not distributed without limit to everyone, as freely as the air we breathe. Nor is it apportioned in equal measure to rich and poor alike. It is not mere coincidence that the primary beneficiaries of Philippine forestry in the Marcos era were presidential cronies and local political bosses, nor that its primary losers were poor Filipinos in general and cultural minorities in particular. Given the distribution of wealth and power in the Philippines, the despoliation of the country's forests was virtually inevitable.

British forester Nicholas Guppy (1984: 944) likens tropical deforestation to a four-layered cake. The topmost layer is population growth and land hunger. Beneath it is the economic order that makes existing agricultural land unavailable to those who need it. Beneath this layer lies the local and national power structure, or what Guppy terms 'political motivations and unwillingness to face realities.' And beneath this is the foundation layer of the deforestation cake: the ready availability of financial backing from external sources that sustains the political *status quo*. Deforestation in the Philippines is a case in point.

The neoclassical prescriptions for market failure are straightforward. Whenever feasible, resources should be privatized and rights to them made secure, so that individuals have an incentive to plan with longer-term time horizons and are compelled to internalize externalities. When this is not feasible, as is often the case, the government should step in to regulate resource use. Both prescriptions presume the existence of a non-partisan, efficiency-maximizing state, the role of which is either to allocate and enforce property rights or to regulate individual behavior.

The political economist recognizes that such states have never existed, and probably never will. The actions of states, whether in creating the preconditions for markets or in redressing market failures, are invariably shaped by the prevailing distribution of power. In a setting of marked political and economic inequalities, one can expect state policies with respect to the natural environment to favor the interests of the rich and powerful over those of the poor and powerless. If environmental degradation benefits the former at the expense of the latter, it will continue until such time as it is blocked by the mobilization of countervailing power. Herein lies the vital link between environmentalism and democracy.

NOTES

1. Roque (1987: 308). Similarly Quisumbing (1987: 1) reports that about 130 holders of logging licenses controlled 33 percent of the country's forest area in the mid-1980s.
2. The politically contingent nature of these rights was vividly demonstrated after the February 1986 revolution, when 150 of the 157 major concession licenses reportedly were revoked within three months (Hurst 1990: 189).
3. A nationwide forest resources inventory conducted from 1979 to 1988 by the Philippine government with German assistance reached similar conclusions. Total forest area as of 1988 was estimated at 6.5 million ha, with average annual loss of 210,000 ha/year (Philippine–German Forest Resources Inventory Project 1988: 3).
4. Japan remained the single largest market despite the fact that its share in the total value of Philippine forestry exports fell from roughly 60 percent in the 1960s to 30 percent in the early 1980s (United Nations, *Foreign Trade Statistics of Asia and the Far East*, various issues). Japan mainly imported logs and lumber, imposing tariffs to product its domestic wood processing industry. As Philippine forest resources dwindled, veneer and plywood

(for which the USA, EU, and Hong Kong are major markets) claimed an increasing share of total Philippine exports, and this contributed to the diminishing Japanese share. See also Takeuchi (1974) and Nectoux and Kuroda (1989).

5. Professor Hans Steinlin, Albert Ludwig University, Freiburg, West Germany, quoted by Caufield (1985b: 155). See also Ledec (1985: 196) and Nectoux and Kuroda (1989: 105–6).

6. The World Bank (1989: 20) reports that extracted wood is 55 percent of total volume reduction, and that a further 30–50 percent is lost in processing, so that total end recovery is one-fifth to one-third of the growing stock reduction. This is compared to recovery rates of 85 percent in both logging and processing in some industrialized countries.

7. Boychuck (1987: 20), citing research conducted by the Manila-based Appropriate Technology Center for Rural Development. See also USAID (1980: 19); Porter and Ganapin (1988: 29); and World Bank (1989: 24–6).

8. The extent to which past prices would have supported sustainable-yield forestry exports is an open question. The United Nations Industrial Development Organization (1983: 338, 349–53) identifies the Philippines as a country with very strong 'revealed comparative advantage' in wood products, indicated by a low ratio of domestic consumption to gross output. However, this calculation ignores the social costs of past forestry practices.

9. Myers (1988) reports that 'there appears to be a timber famine in the making' in the Philippines. The President of the Philippine Wood Products Association predicted in 1986 that the country would have to import logs from Malaysia in coming years (cited by Hurst 1990: 170).

10. USAID (1985: 21–2). For a review of soil erosion estimation problems, see David (1984: 18–25). David's estimates for the Magat reservoir watershed in northern Luzon indicate that soil loss rates range from 3 mt/ha/year from primary forests with small patches of clearings to 250 mt/ha/year from overgrazed areas.

11. Caufield (1985b: 24) states that Ambuklao's operational life span was reduced to 30 years. USAID (1979: 70) states that siltation reduced the useful life of the dam from 60 years to 32 years.

12. World Bank (1989: 27). See also Myers (1988: 208).

13. FAO and UNDP, 'Watershed problems and status of watershed management: country brief, Philippines,' FAO:RAS/81/053, June 1982, p. 10, cited by Porter and Ganapin (1988: 24).

14. The World Resources Institute (1990: 15) estimates, for example, that the United States accounted for 17.6 percent of the world's net greenhouse gas emissions in 1987, while the Philippines accounted for 0.7 percent. On a per capita basis, US emissions were more than six times higher than those of the Philippines (calculated from World Resources Institute 1991: 254–5, 348–9). Moreover, these estimates have been criticized for *understating* the share of the industrialized countries and *overstating* that of the developing countries (see Agarwal and Narain 1990). See also Kellogg and Schware (1982: 1080) and references therein.

15. Whitmore (1984: 288). Whitmore notes (p. 6), however, that forests of comparable richness may yet be discovered in Latin America.

16. See, for example, Tietenberg (1988: 49–53).

17. The latter problem is often described as the 'tragedy of the commons,' but as Bromley and Cernea (1989) point out, it is more accurately termed the tragedy of *open access*, since collective action can, and often does, result in socially rational use of common property resources.

18. For details, see Aguilar (1982: 154–6); Anti-Slavery Society (1983: 74–90); Hurst (1990: 194–6); Nectoux and Kuroda (1989: 84–5); and Porter and Ganapin (1988: 27).

19. See Porter and Ganapin (1988: 25) and Roth (1983).

20. For details, see Tadem *et al.* (1984: 104–45) and Anti-Slavery Society (1983: ch. 4).

21. Quoted by Hurst (1990: 189).

22. Power and Tumaneng (1983: 8). See also Nectoux and Kuroda (1989: 71–3).

23. Moore (1910: 150), cited by Roth (1983: 46).

24. Boado (1988: 184). 'Granted that the government's capture might have been higher by

another 5 percent owing to unaccounted domestic sales and realty taxes,' Boado (p. 185) concludes, 'the profit margin of the timber operators would still remain high.' The World Bank (1989: 146–7) cites similar figures. See also Power and Tumaneng (1983).

25. J.B. Alvarez, Jr, 'Forests and rural communities,' paper presented at the Integrated Natural Resources Symposium, Manila, July 1982, quoted by Porter and Ganapin (1988: 28).
26. For details, see Clad and Vitug (1988).
27. In 1987, the World Bank, like the BFD, vowed to reform. 'If the World Bank has been part of the problem in the past,' Bank president Barber Conable proclaimed in a speech on the environment, 'it can and will be a strong force in finding solutions in the future' (quoted by Rich 1989: 73). This declaration came in the wake of vigorous campaigning by environmental organizations, including well-publicized demonstrations at the World Bank's Washington headquarters. 'They're scaling the walls at the Bank!' a senior consultant told me. 'On the outside, not on the inside like we used to do.'
28. Anti-Slavery Society (1983: 79); Bello *et al.* (1982: 89–90). When entering the Tinggian lands, Cellophil personnel were 'accompanied and guarded by elements of Marcos's special Presidential Guard Battalion' (Anti-Slavery Society 1983: 77).
29. Olofson (1981: 3), cited by Lopez (1987: 230). Shifting cultivators are referred to in official documents as *kaigineros*, which Tadem *et al.* (1984) consider a disparaging term for tribal Filipinos and settlers. For a discussion of differences between the agricultural practices of traditional swidden cultivators and those of the migrant settlers, see Fujisaka and Sajise (1986) and Hurst (1990: 184–5).
30. Cruz *et al.* (1986: 39–49) estimate that 'upland population' grew from an estimated 8.2 million in 1960 to 14.4 million in 1980, maintaining a fairly constant share of 30 percent in the country's total population. The Bureau of Forestry Development estimated upland population in the early 1980s at 7.5 million (Capistrano and Fujisaka 1984: 2).
31. For a review of the government policies with respect to cultural minorities in the Marcos years, see Anti-Slavery Society (1983).
32. Owen Lynch, Jr, quoted by Poffenberger (1990: 12).
33. See Lynch (1984: 187) and Lynch and Talbot (1988: 686).
34. P.D. 705, section 53, quoted in Anti-Slavery Society (1983: 67).
35. Porter and Ganapin (1988: 29). For example, attempts to award stewardship certificates under the World Bank-assisted Central Visayas Regional Project foundered, among other reasons, on the opposition from *de facto* landlords who 'fear loss of revenue generated by illegal land claims' (Reid *et al.* 1988: 31).
36. Moreover, in some cases certificate holders are reported to 'lease out portions of the land grants to other farmers with minuscule farms or to the landless' (Cornista 1985: 6).
37. Natonton and Abraham (1984: 121). For contrasting views of a lumber company's activities, compare this account to that of Tadem *et al.* (1984: 138–45).
38. See, for example, Ooi (1987). In a cross-sectional analysis of Philippine provinces, however, Kummer (1992) finds no significant correlation between population growth and the loss of forest cover from 1970 to 1980.
39. Letter to F.A. Lange, 29 March 1865, quoted by Baran (1957: 242). Emphasis in original.
40. The Philippines is not unique in this respect. See, for example, Guppy (1984: 939–44) on Brazil and Indonesia.
41. For further discussion of the country's agrarian structure and of the failure of its debt-led industrialization strategy, see Boyce (1993).
42. Quoted by Clad (1988) and by Lynch and Talbot (1988: 680).
43. This and other examples of grassroots environmental movements in the Philippines are discussed by Lynch and Talbot (1988: 702–9).
44. See Broad and Cavanagh (1989, 1993). For examples from other countries, see Durning (1990).
45. A parallel story could be related for the country's mining sector. See McAndrew (1983) and Briones (1987).

REFERENCES

Agarwal, A. and Narain, S. (1990), *Global Warming in an Unequal World*, New Delhi: Centre for Science and Environment.

Aguilar, F., Jr (1982), *Social Forestry for Upland Development: Lessons from Four Case Studies*, Quezon City: Institute of Philippine Culture.

Alvarez, J.B., Jr (1987), 'DNR [Department of Natural Resources] tenure program in the public domain,' paper presented at the Workshop on the Accelerated Agrarian Reform Program, University of the Philippines, Diliman, 11–12 March.

Anderson, J.N. (1987), 'Lands at risk, people at risk: Perspectives on tropical forest transformation in the Philippines,' in P.D. Little and M.M. Horowitz (eds), *Lands at Risk in the Third World: Local Level Perspectives*, Boulder, CO: Westview Press, pp. 249–67.

Anti-Slavery Society (1983), *The Philippines: Authoritarian Government, Multinationals and Ancestral Lands*, Indigenous Peoples and Development Series, Report no. 1, London: Anti-Slavery Society.

Asian Development Bank (1987), *A Review of Forestry and Forest Industries in the Asia Pacific Region*, Manila: ADB, Agriculture Department.

Baran, P. (1957), *The Political Economy of Growth*, New York: Monthly Review.

Bello, W., Kinley, D. and Elinson, E. (1982), *Development Debacle: The World Bank in the Philippines*, Makati: Philippine Institute for Development Studies.

Boado, E.L. (1988), 'Incentive policies and forest use in the Philippines,' in R. Repetto and M. Gillis (eds), *Public Policies and the Misuse of Forest Resources*, Cambridge: Cambridge University Press, pp. 165–203.

Borlagdan, S.B. (1990), 'Social forestry in upland Cebu,' in M. Poffenberger (ed), *Keepers of the Forest: Land Management Alternatives in Southeast Asia*, West Hartford, CT: Kumarian Press, pp. 266–76.

Boyce, J.K. (1993), *The Philippines: The Political Economy of Growth and Impoverishment in the Marcos Era*, London: Macmillan; Honolulu: University of Hawaii Press; and Quezon City: Ateneo de Manila University Press.

Boychuck, R. (1987), 'Exodus of the hungry: The environmental consequences of rural poverty in the Philippines,' mimeo, London, September.

Briones, N.D. (1987), 'Mining pollution: The case of the Baguio mining district, the Philippines,' *Environmental Management*, 11(3): 335–44.

Broad, R. and Cavanagh, J. (1989), 'Marcos's ghost,' *Amicus Journal* (Washington, DC: Natural Resources Defense Council), 11(4): 18–29.

Broad, R. and Cavanagh, J. (1993), *Plundering Paradise: The Struggle for the Environment in the Philippines*, Berkeley, CA: University of California Press.

Bromley, D.W. and Cernea, M.M. (1989), 'The management of common property resources,' Discussion Paper no. 57, Washington, DC: World Bank.

Capistrano, A.D. and Fujisaka, S. (1984), 'Tenure, technology, and productivity of agroforestry schemes,' Philippine Institute for Development Studies Working Paper no. 84–06.

Caufield, C. (1985a), 'A reporter at large: The rain forests,' *New Yorker*, 14 January: 41–101.

Caufield, C. (1985b), *In the Rainforest*, New York: Alfred W. Knopf.

Clad, J. (1988), 'The fragile forests: Church pastoral letter protests against despoliation,' *Far Eastern Economic Review*, 25 February: 19.

Clad, J. and Vitug, M.D. (1988), 'The politics of plunder: Palawan's forests appear doomed in a power struggle,' *Far Eastern Economic Review*, 24 November: 48–52.

Cornista, L.B. (1985), 'Land tenure system in the Philippine uplands: Its implications to agroforestry,' Seminar Paper no. 1, Los Banos: University of the Philippines, Agrarian Reform Institute.

Crewdson, J. (1986), 'Marcos graft staggering: Investigators trace billions in holdings,' *Chicago Tribune*, 23 March: 1, 20–1.

Cruz, M.C.J., Zosa-Feranil, I. and Goce, C.L. (1986), 'Population pressure and migration: Implications for upland development in the Philippines,' Working Paper no. 86-06, Los Banos: UPLB, Center for Policy and Development Studies.

David, W.P. (1984), 'Environmental effects of watershed modifications,' Working Paper 84-07, Manila: Philippine Institute for Development Studies.

Durning, A. (1990), 'Environmentalism South,' *Amicus Journal* (Washington, DC: Natural Resources Defense Council), 12(3): 12–18.

Food and Agriculture Organization (1977), *1975 Yearbook of Forest Products*, Rome: FAO.

Fujisaka, S. and Sajise, P. (1986), 'Change and "development" in the uplands: A synthesis of lessons, unresolved issues, and implications,' in S. Fujisaka, P.E. Sajise and R.A. del Castillo (eds), *Man, Agriculture, and the Tropical Forest: Change and Development in the Philippine Uplands*, Bangkok: Winrock International Institute for Agricultural Development, pp. 337–60.

Guppy, N. (1984), 'Tropical deforestation: A global view,' *Foreign Affairs*, 62(4): 928–65.

Hurst, P. (1990), *Rainforest Politics: Ecological Destruction in South-East Asia*. London: Zed Books.

Kellogg W. and Schware, R. (1982), 'Society, science, and climate change,' *Foreign Affairs*, 60(5): 1076–110.

Kramer, B. (1978), 'Ties to the top: In the Philippines, it's whom you know that can really count,' *Wall Street Journal*, 12 January: 1, 18.

Kummer, D.M. (1992), *Deforestation in the Post-War Philippines*, Chicago: University of Chicago Press.

Laarman, J.G. (1988), 'Export of tropical hardwoods in the twentieth century,' in J.F. Richards and R.P. Tucker (eds), *World Deforestation in the Twentieth Century*, Durham, NC: Duke University Press, pp. 147–63.

Ledec, G. (1985), 'The political economy of tropical deforestation,' in H.J. Leonard (ed), *Divesting Nature's Capital: The Political Economy of Environmental Abuse in the Third World*, New York: Holmes & Meier, pp. 179–226.

Lopez , M.E. (1987), 'The politics of land at risk in a Philippine frontier,' in P.D. Little and M.M. Horowitz (eds), *Lands at Risk in the Third World: Local Level Perspectives*, Boulder, CO: Westview Press, pp. 230–48.

Lynch, O., Jr (1984), 'Withered roots and landgrabbers: A survey of research on upland tenure and displacement,' in C.P. Castro (ed), *Uplands and Uplanders: In Search of New Perspectives*, Quezon City: Bureau of Forest Development, Upland Development Program, pp. 167–230.

Lynch, O., Jr, and Talbot, K. (1988), 'Legal responses to the Philippine deforestation crisis,' *New York University Journal of International Law and Politics*, 20(3): 679–713.

Mackenzie, D. (1988), 'Uphill battle to save Filipino trees,' *New Scientist*, 30 June: 42–3.

McAndrew, J.P. (1983), *The Impact of Corporate Mining of Local Philippine Communities*, Davao City: Alternate Resource Center.

McCue, A. (1982), 'Philippines facing economic disaster as villagers, loggers denude hillsides,' *Wall Street Journal*, 27 April.

Moore, B. (1910), 'Forest problems in the Philippines,' *American Forestry*, 16 (February and March): 75–81, 149–54.

Myers, N. (1988), 'Environmental degradation and some economic consequences in the Philippines,' *Environmental Conservation*, 15(3): 205–14.

Natonton, J. and Abraham, F.B., Jr (1984), 'Regenerated forest in Agusan,' in *The Key to Philippine Forest Conservation: The Defense of the Dipterocarps*, Manila: Columbian Publishing Corporation, pp. 100–24.

Nectoux, F. and Kuroda Y. (1989), *Timber from the South Seas: An Analysis of Japan's Tropical Timber Trade and its Environmental Impact*, Gland, Switzerland: WWF International (World Wildlife Fund for Nature).

Olofson, H. (1981), 'Introduction,' in H. Olofson (ed), *Adaptive Strategies and Change in Philippine Swidden-based Societies*, Laguna: Forest Field Report Series no. 18.

Ooi, J.B. (1987), *Depletion of Forest Resources in the Philippines*, Field Report Series no. 18, Singapore: Institute of Southeast Asian Studies, ASEAN Economic Research Unit.

Organization for Economic Cooperation and Development (1991), *Environmental Indicators: A Preliminary Set*, Paris: OECD.

Philippine–German Forest Resources Inventory Project (1988), *Natural Forest Resources of the Philippines*, Manila: Department of Environment and Natural Resources, Forest Management Bureau.

Poffenberger, M. (1990), 'The evolution of forestry management systems in Southeast Asia,' in M. Poffenberger (ed), *Keepers of the Forest: Land Management Alternatives in Southeast Asia*, West Hartford, CT: Kumarian Press, pp. 7–26.

Porter, G. and Ganapin, D., Jr (1988), *Resources, Population, and the Philippines' Future: A Case Study*, Washington, DC: World Resources Institute.

Power, J.H. and Tumaneng, T.D. (1983), 'Comparative advantage and government price intervention policies in forestry,' Working Paper no. 83-05, Manila: Philippine Institute for Development Studies.

Quisumbing, M.A. (1987), 'Land reform for forest and upland areas: Some suggestions,' Los Banos: UPLB, Department of Economics, mimeo, May.

Raven, P.H. (1987), *The Global Ecosystem in Crisis*, Chicago: MacArthur Foundation.

Reid, W.V., Barnes, J.N. and Blackwelder, B. (1988), *Bankrolling Successes: A Portfolio of Sustainable Development Projects*, Washington, DC: Environmental Policy Institute and National Wildlife Federation.

Repetto, R. (1988), 'Nature's resources as productive assets,' *Challenge*, 32(5): 16–20.

Revilla, A.V., Jr (1984), 'Forest land management in the context of national land use,' Working Paper no. 84-02, Manila: Philippine Institute for Development Studies.

Reyes, M.R. (1984), 'Perpetuating the Dipterocarp forest in productive condition,' in *The Key to Philippine Forest Conservation: Defense of the Dipterocarps*, Manila: Columbian Publishing Corporation, pp. 28–60.

Rich, B. (1989), 'Funding deforestation: Conservation woes at the World Bank,' *Nation* (New York), 23 January: 73, 88–91.

Roque, C.R. (1987), 'Environmental futures of the Philippines,' in F.S. Jose (ed), *A Filipino Agenda for the 21st Century*, Manila: Solidaridad, pp. 305–17.

Roth, D. (1983), 'Philippine forests and forestry, 1595–1920,' in R. Tucker and J.F.

Richards (eds), *Global Deforestation and the Nineteenth Century World Economy*, Durham, NC: Duke University Press, pp. 30–49.

Scott, M. (1989), 'The disappearing forests,' *Far Eastern Economic Review*, 12 January: 34–8.

Tadem, E.C., Reyes, J. and Magno, L.S. (1984), *Showcases of Underdevelopment: Fishes, Forests, and Fruits*, Davao City: Alternate Resource Center.

Takeuchi, K. (1974), *Tropical Hardwoods Trade in the Asia Pacific Region*, World Bank Staff Occasional Paper no. 17, Baltimore, MD: Johns Hopkins University Press.

Tietenberg, T. (1988), *Environmental and Natural Resource Economics*, 2nd edn., Glenview, IL: Scott, Foresman.

United Nations Industrial Development Organization (UNIDO) (1983), *Industry in a Changing World*, New York: United Nations.

United States Agency for International Development (USAID) (1979), *Environmental and Natural Resource Management in Developing Countries: A Report to Congress*, vol. I, Washington, DC: USAID, February.

—— (1980), *Country Development Strategy Statement, FY 1982: Philippines*, Manila: USAID, January.

—— (1985), *County Development Strategy Statement, FY 1986–90:USAID/Philippines*, Washington, DC: USAID, March; abridged version, April 1986.

Whitmore, T.C. (1984), *Tropical Rainforests of the Far East*, Oxford: Clarendon Press.

World Bank (1962), *Economic Growth in the Philippines: A Preliminary Report Prepared by the Staff of the IBRD*, 4 January; published as *Appendix II to the State of the Nation Message of President Diosdado Macapagal*, 22 January.

World Bank (1973), *Current Economic Position and Prospects of the Philippines*, vol. I, 20 April, Report no. 78-PH, Washington, DC: World Bank.

World Bank (1989), *Philippines: Forestry, Fisheries, and Agricultural Resource Management Study*, Report no. 7388-PH, 17 January; subsequently published as *Philippines: Environment and Natural Resource Management Study*, Washington, DC: World Bank.

World Resources Institute (1990), *World Resources 1990–91*, New York: Oxford University Press.

Zablan, F.M. (1961), 'Binga hydroelectric project,' *Indian Journal of Power and River Valley Development*, 11(4): 1–10.

9. Democratizing environmental ownership

A central theme in this book has been the intimate connection between how people treat each other and how they treat the environment. One way in which people wield power over others is by imposing environmental costs on them. To be sure, this is not normally done for its own sake. In most cases – with the notable exception of warfare – poisoning other people's air or water and diminishing their natural resource base is not an end in itself, but simply a side-effect of the pursuit of the usual economic aims of production and consumption at the least cost. The costs that producers and consumers seek to minimize, however, are not *total* costs, but only the *internal* costs they bear themselves. The ability of economic actors to impose external costs on others, thereby reducing their own internal costs, depends on the relative power of those who generate pollution and resource depletion *vis-à-vis* those on the receiving end of these costs. When the power disparity between them is wide, we can expect more environmental degradation than when the disparity is narrow.

This link, between the power to abuse other people and the power to abuse the environment, suggests that *democratization*, in the broad sense of movement toward a more equal distribution of power, can promote environmental protection. This is not to say that democracy offers a panacea for environmental ills, or that the strength of environmental policy depends only on the strength of democracy. The values and preferences of citizens matter, too. If no one objects to breathing dirty air, democratization will not change the extent of air pollution. More realistically, perhaps, if the current generation does not care about the well-being of future generations, then a more democratic distribution of power today may not suffice to safeguard the environment for those to follow.[1]

Nor does the link between power disparities and environmental degradation imply that efforts to protect the environment must take a back seat to efforts to build a more democratic society. On the contrary, the two tasks often go together. The principle that all persons have an inalienable 'right to a clean and healthful environment' not only provides a rationale for environmental protection, but also extends the terrain of democracy itself.[2] It embraces a profoundly egalitarian vision of what can be termed 'environmental ownership,' where 'ownership' is understood not as unbridled license to do whatever one pleases, but rather as a right tempered by responsibility.

This chapter pursues this theme. First, I distinguish between democratization on the one hand, and changes in the state–market mix in economic policy on the other, arguing that these are distinct dimensions of social organization. Next I examine some links between property rights and democracy, a longstanding concern of political economists. Finally, I consider strategies for democratizing environmental ownership by building natural assets in the hands of low-income individuals and communities, so as to advance the goals of poverty reduction, environmental protection, and environmental justice.

STATES AND MARKETS

The degree to which a society deserves to be called 'democratic' or the opposite, 'oligarchic,' does not hinge on whether it accords a bigger role in economic affairs to the market or to the state. Both states and markets function democratically when power and wealth are widely diffused; both function oligarchically when power and wealth are concentrated in few hands.

Real-world societies lie between the hypothetical extremes of pure democracy (here taken to mean a perfectly equal distribution of power) and pure oligarchy (or absolute dictatorship). At the same time, real-world societies lie somewhere between the theoretical poles of an economy governed solely by the market or solely by the state. These two continuums – the degree of democracy, and state–market mix – describe different dimensions of society (see Figure 9.1). In the nineteenth and twentieth centuries, the contending ideologies of 'right' and 'left' often sought to collapse them into a single axis,

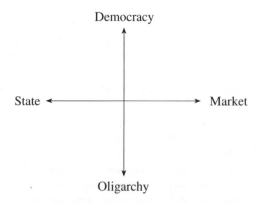

Figure 9.1   Two continuums: Democracy–oligarchy and market–state

the right identifying democracy with the market and oligarchy with the state, and the left making the opposite equation.[3] Yet whichever way the axes were rotated, history has shown that neither the market nor the state automatically guarantees democracy.

In the arena of environmental policy, in the past two decades it has become fashionable among economists to advocate tradable emission permits – pollution allowances that can be bought and sold – as a market-based alternative to 'command-and-control' pollution regulations. The creation of such permits can be seen as a movement along the state–market continuum in the direction of the market. In 1990, for example, the United States Congress established tradable permits for sulfur dioxide (SO_2) emissions, a health hazard and a major cause of acid rain. Aiming to cut total SO_2 emissions to less than half their 1980 level by the year 2000, the government issued a fixed number of permits to electric power companies, which they then could trade among themselves; in 1999, the market price for SO_2 permits was roughly $125 per ton of emissions (Goodstein 1999: 321). Firms that are able to cut emissions more cheaply than buying a permit will do so, while firms for which emissions reductions are more costly will buy permits. This flexibility, compared to the usual one-rule-fits-all approach to pollution regulation, is intended to achieve the overall pollution-reduction target at the least total cost.

Permit-trading schemes have certain drawbacks compared to regulations: in particular, the administrative costs of monitoring compliance are likely to be higher when firms can choose different levels and methods of pollution control, and the clustering of permits in specific geographical areas can lead to pollution 'hot spots' even as national or regional targets are met. The balance between these pros and cons of regulations and tradable permits is likely to vary from case to case.

Is one alternative, however, intrinsically more democratic than the other? Some 'free-market environmentalists,' axiomatically identifying markets with democracy, champion tradable emission permits on this basis. Yet the degree to which a pollution permit scheme is genuinely democratic depends on how it is implemented: how pollution targets are set and how permits are distributed. If the public is well-informed about the extent and impacts of pollution and is actively involved in defining pollution-reduction goals, and if safeguards are put in place to prevent the emergence of local hot spots that concentrate high levels of pollution in specific communities, then a permit-trading scheme is more democratic than if these conditions are not met. If the permits are auctioned periodically and the proceeds shared equally among the citizens, the scheme is more democratic than if the permits are handed out free-of-charge to polluters, as happened with SO_2 permits in the USA. By the same token, the extent to which pollution regulations are democratic likewise depends on the degree of public participation in decision making and on how the costs and benefits of regulation are distributed.

Of course, tradable emission permits are not a creature of the market alone. Government action is needed to create the permits and to enforce compliance with their terms. In the absence of these interventions, the market fails to provide adequate incentives for environmental protection. Yet government failure can be just as serious as market failure: there is no guarantee that the state will 'do the right thing,' faithfully calibrating its interventions to serve the public good. Just as the market responds to price signals founded on a given distribution of wealth and income, the state responds to political signals founded on a given distribution of power. Hence it is no accident that government policies undertaken in the name of the national interest often bring disproportionate benefits to the nation's most powerful people.

Democratic accountability grounded in an equitable distribution of power and wealth is the only reliable way to channel government interventions toward the public interest rather than private interests, and toward correction of market failures rather than their further exacerbation. The results will be as imperfect as democracy itself, but they are likely to be superior to the practical alternatives. As Winston Churchill once observed, 'Democracy is the worst form of government – except all those other forms that have been tried.' In framing environmental policy, the challenge therefore is not simply to strike the right balance between states and markets – important as this may be – but also to ensure that the policy mix is chosen and implemented democratically.

PROPERTY RIGHTS AS ENDS AND MEANS

A long tradition in western political thought maintains that property rights and democracy go hand-in-hand. Democracy protects citizens against usurpation of their property rights by a political elite; widely dispersed property ownership protects democracy against subordination to an economic elite. This mutually supportive relationship rests on an egalitarian base: all citizens have the right to vote, all have the right to own property. Moreover, for democracy to flourish the citizens not only must hold these rights in theory but also must exercise them in practice. When the ownership of wealth is highly concentrated, the mutually supportive relationship between property rights and democracy is supplanted by one of tension, as the rich seek to translate their economic muscle into political dominance and the poor seek to use their political majority to wrest economic gains.

A longstanding debate in United States jurisprudence pits two opposing conceptions of property rights against each other. The first is a 'sanctified' conception in which property rights can and should be perfectly defined and perfectly secure; its proponents regard the upholding of these unambiguous property rights as the central purpose of the state. The second is an 'instrumental' conception in which property rights are regarded as a tool to pursue more fundamental social aims, such as efficiency, growth, and justice.[4] Both schools of thought acknowledge that property rights are socially constructed – creations of human law, not divine ordination – but proponents of the sanctified view tend to see this as an accomplished fact, while proponents of the instrumental view see it as an open-ended historical process.

The sanctified view thus holds that property rights are an end, both in the historical sense that their construction has been completed and in the normative sense that their protection is a basic end-in-itself. The instrumental view, by contrast, holds that property rights are malleable, changing along with values, technology, and institutions, and that they are a means toward a society's other ends.

The mainstream view of property rights in United States law has been firmly in the instrumental camp. With the abolition of slavery in the mid-nineteenth century, for example, the triumph of anti-slavery ethics led to 'one of history's largest expropriations of property' (Friedman 2001: 5). In 1877 the US Supreme Court explicitly declared in the case *Munn* v. *Illinois* that 'a government may regulate the conduct of its citizens toward each other, and, when necessary for the public good, the manner in which each shall use his own property.' In the late twentieth century, Congress and the state governments redefined property rights to further the social goals of environmental protection and occupational health and safety.

In recent decades, however, proponents of 'free-market environmentalism' have argued not only for more reliance on market-based instruments for environmental protection, but also for a sanctified view of property rights. Any new regulations that limit what firms or individuals can do with property are depicted as 'takings' for which property owners deserve compensation from the government. In this view, property rights are already perfectly defined: any rights not withheld by prior legislation, or legally held by others, rest with the landowner. The right to drain and build on wetlands, for example, is not explicitly granted by law, but any government actions to protect wetlands is seen as taking these rights from the landowner – a default setting that dismisses the rights of others to the water regulation and wildlife habitat services provided by these ecosystems. This line of reasoning conveniently ignores the extent to which private property in the United States is founded on past takings, notably from Native Americans. It also ignores the extent to which current property values are enhanced by proximity to publicly funded roads and other infrastructure, 'givings' for which governments typically are not compensated by the property owners who benefit.[5]

In effect, the demand for 'takings' compensation is a 'demand to be paid for no longer being allowed to undertake activities now declared to be illegal' (Bromley 1993: 672). Laws generally do impinge on people's ability to do whatever they wish – otherwise they would be unnecessary – and in some cases this reduces the value of a property below what it would otherwise fetch. The view that landowners ought to be compensated for such losses presumes not only that property rights are already perfectly specified, so that any change constitutes an infringement on their prior rights rather than a clarification of imperfectly defined and competing claims, but also that the entire legal and regulatory framework has been perfectly specified, too, insofar as it affects property values.

Acceptance of the principle that property owners ought to be compensated for any adverse impacts of new laws and regulations on property values would turn legislation into something closer to a market exchange – a dramatic movement on the state–market axis. At the same time, it would resolve existing and future conflicts over environmental ownership in favor of the parties already best-endowed with property rights. In place of the 'polluter pays principle,' that demands payment from the users of environmental sinks, it would allocate the right to pollute to property owners: if anti-pollution regulations diminish their property values, the public must compensate them. In place of the principle that the public has a right to the ecosystem services, such as those provided by wetlands, the 'takings' proponents would require the public to pay landowners to protect these services.

A democratic society requires checks not only on the power of state, but also on the power of private firms and individuals to advance their self-interest at the expense of the public interest. The sanctification of private property rights would address the first need but not the second. The democratization of environmental ownership, based on the principle that all people have a right to a clean and healthy environment, would address both. In doing so, it would build on the instrumental tradition in which property rights are a means to an end, rather than an end in themselves.

In practice, property rights are reallocated and redefined over time. Reallocation can lead to a more equitable distribution of wealth or to greater concentration of wealth. Redefinition can protect the environment or accelerate environmental degradation. The results are not a foregone conclusion, but chapters in an unfinished history, the outcomes of which are shaped by the distribution of power, and at the same time help to reshape it.

BUILDING NATURAL ASSETS

In recent years, there has been growing recognition that poverty is not simply a lack of income today, but also results from a lack of assets that will yield income and other benefits tomorrow.[6] Increases in the asset base of the poor – their financial, physical, human, and natural capital – are critical for lasting reductions in poverty. Democratizing access to natural resources and environmental sinks can be an important component of asset-building strategies for poverty reduction.

There are four main routes for building natural assets in the hands of low-income communities and individuals: (a) *investment*, the creation of new natural capital, or the increases in the stocks of natural capital to which the poor already have access; (b) *redistribution*, the transfer of natural capital from others to the poor; (c) *internalization*, increases in the ability of the poor to capture benefits flowing from natural capital they already own; and (d) *appropriation*, the establishment of egalitarian rights to open-access resources (see Table 9.1). The first two routes, investment and redistribution, are applicable to many other types of assets; the latter two routes, internalization and appropriation, are based on special features of natural assets.

Table 9.1   Routes to natural asset-building

Route	Definition	Examples
Investment	The creation of new natural capital, or the increase of existing natural capital.	Incentives for soil conservation directed to small farmers.
Redistribution	The transfer of natural capital from others.	The granting of the power of eminent domain over vacant lots in inner cities to community organizations.
Internalization	The provision of compensation for previously uncompensated benefits to others that flow from a person's stewardship of natural assets.	Rewarding small farmers for their role in the conservation of crop genetic diversity, or small forest owners for their role in watershed management.
Appropriation	The establishment of rights to what have previously been open-access resources.	The mobilization of communities to combat industrial pollution of the air they breathe and the water they drink.

Investment

In recent years, the dismal notion that human activity inexorably depreciates natural capital – our only choice being how rapidly to do so – has given way to a more positive vision based on the recognition that humans can invest in natural capital (see, for example, Jansson *et al.* 1994). Such investment offers one route to expand the natural asset base of the poor, a route that is particularly relevant in cases where the poor already own or have access to natural assets whose quantity and quality can be augmented.

The soil and water conservation programs of the US Department of Agriculture, for example, aim to support investments in natural capital. Historically, however, these government programs often have discriminated against low-income and minority farmers.[7] If this pattern were reversed – that is, if government support were preferentially directed to these farmers, instead of away from them – such programs could form part of a natural asset-building strategy for the reduction of rural poverty.

More generally, many of the world's poor, particularly in rural Asia, Africa, and Latin America, rely on natural resources for their livelihoods, but suffer from 'ecological poverty' in that their resource base has been degraded (Agarwal and Narain 2000). In such settings, investments in ecological restoration can go hand-in-hand with poverty reduction.

Redistribution

Redistribution is particularly relevant to non-renewable resources such as land and minerals, the supply of which cannot be increased by investment. Land reform – the transfer of rights from large landowners to tenant farmers and landless laborers – was a key element in the successful post-World War II economic development strategies of countries such as China, Taiwan, and Korea. The potential for redistribution is not limited, however, to the agricultural sectors of developing countries. In inner-city Boston, for example, a community-based organization called the Dudley Street Neighborhood Initiative won the right to redevelop vacant lots in the late 1980s, an example of urban land reform (Medoff and Sklar 1994).

Property rights are often described as a 'bundle of sticks' composed of different rights to the same piece of property. A farmer, for example, may own the surface rights to a tract of land, while a coal company owns rights to the minerals beneath it, and the air overhead is an open-access resource.[8] Redistribution can involve specific sticks rather than the whole bundle. Land reforms, for example, can give tenants 'occupancy rights' – the right to till the land, without threat of eviction, in return for a legally specified share of the crop – rather than full title to the land. Similarly, in the reclamation and redevelopment of urban 'brownfields' in the USA, some local communities have secured rights to participate in land-use decisions and to share in the resulting employment opportunities, without obtaining full ownership of the redeveloped land (Dixon 2001).

Internalization

When low-income people own natural assets that generate benefits to others, but currently receive no reward for providing these benefits, internalization offers another route to asset-building. For example, crop genetic diversity, sustained by small farmers such as the Mexican *campesinos* described in Chapter 7, represents an immensely valuable global public good. It underpins long-term food security worldwide, providing the raw material for crop adaptations to newly emerging pests and plant diseases and to the changing climate. Yet the farmers who provide this vital service today receive no compensation for doing so. Policies to reward them for these 'positive externalities' – in effect, to internalize some of the benefits that flow from their stewardship of natural assets – could help sustain both their livelihoods and crucial biological resources.

Similarly, small farmers and woodlot owners in the watersheds that serve metropolitan areas can provide important ecological services by regulating the quantity and quality of water that flows from their land. In effect, they are involved in two sorts of production at the same time: they raise crops, livestock, and timber for sale on the market or domestic use, and they provide water for downstream users. The problem is that landowners are rewarded for the first activity but not for the second, with predictable effects on their priorities. Rather than seeking to provide clean and stable water supplies, many landowners produce contaminated or unstable water supplies as a by-product of their agricultural or forestry activities. Again, mechanisms to reward them for providing ecological services would raise their incomes and strengthen their incentives to protect the environment.

Appropriation

Appropriation, the final route to natural asset building, pertains specifically to open-access resources. Since these resources are nobody's property, they are vulnerable to the 'tragedies of open access' discussed in Chapter 1: resource degradation due to overuse, and inequitable distribution due to appropriation by the powerful.

The democratic allocation of rights to these resources could address both tragedies. For example, Peter Barnes and Marc Breslow (2001) have proposed the creation of a 'sky trust' in the United States that would allocate rights to skyborne carbon storage – hitherto an open-access resource – on an egalitarian basis. The trust would receive revenues from charges for carbon emissions, and every year these would be disbursed to every woman, man, and child in the country on an equal per capita basis. Low-income households, who typically consume less fossil fuels (and less of most things) than upper-income households, would pay less into the fund, but everyone would receive the same payout per person. The net effect would be a progressive redistribution of income.[9] In a similar vein, Baer *et al.* (2000) argue that a comprehensive global agreement to reduce greenhouse gas emissions must be based on 'equal rights to the atmospheric commons for every individual' worldwide.

Community struggles against air and water pollution provide an example of natural asset-building via the appropriation route: in effect, these communities are claiming rights to environmental 'sinks' that in the past were treated as open-access resources. The benefits to communities that secure these rights include better health, improved environmental quality, and higher property values.

In principle, the establishment of community-based rights to local airsheds and water bodies could also generate income in the form of compensation for whatever pollution the community accepts within the bounds set by environmental regulations. Such compensation – an application of the 'polluter pays principle' – need not imply that regulatory standards should be relaxed or abandoned; on the contrary, it would reinforce the pollution-control impact of existing standards by making polluters pay for their use of environmental sinks within legal limits.

In practice, these four routes to natural asset-building often overlap. Forestry stewardship initiatives, for example, can combine investment in forest management with the internalization of benefits from ecosystem services.[10] Brownfields redevelopment can combine the appropriation of the right to a clean environment, the redistribution of property rights (or certain sticks in the property-rights bundle) from absentee landlords to community-based organizations, and investment in cleanup and new development. Alone and in combination, such strategies can simultaneously advance the goals of poverty reduction, environmental protection, and environmental justice.

CONCLUSION

In the face of environmental degradation and social injustice, it is all too easy to succumb to a sense of despair. The gap between what is possible and what exists, and the resulting sacrifices in well-being for current and future generations, are painful to contemplate. This book does not minimize these realities, nor does it offer quick and easy solutions. Yet the analysis presented here carries a message of hope.

If the impact of human activity on nature is not inevitably negative, but can also be positive – as illustrated by the domestication of crops and animals and their ongoing evolution over several thousand years – then there is hope for sustainable advances in human well-being.

If our willingness to abuse the environment is founded on our ability to abuse each other, then we can strengthen the social foundation for environmental protection by acting to reduce the disparities of power and wealth that foster such abuses.

If we have the maturity and humility to appreciate how much our well-being today rests on the hard work and wisdom of the generations that preceded us, then we can appreciate our own profound responsibilities to the future generations that will follow us.

These are hopes, not certainties. But they are more than wishful thinking. The possibility for a more democratic and environmentally sustainable future builds upon the struggles and victories of past generations, who have confronted challenges just as formidable as those we face today. Much has happened in the 400 generations since humans invented agriculture. Only ten generations ago, hereditary monarchs and aristocracies still ruled much of the world. Only six generations ago, millions of Americans lived in slavery, and the vision of free public education was so radical that it featured among the demands of Karl Marx in *The Communist Manifesto*. Four generations ago, women had yet to win the right to vote in most countries in the world, including the United States. Two generations ago, environmental protection agencies had not been established. Today, as we face the challenges of a new century, we can look to history for both a sense of perspective and a sense of hope.

Just as the earth is our common home, the quest for a democratic and environmentally sustainable society is the common task of humankind. 'Human progress never rolls in on wheels of inevitability,' Martin Luther King, Jr (1965) observed. 'It comes through the tireless efforts and the persistent work of dedicated individuals.' Whether we succeed in building a world founded on respect for the environment and respect for each other will depend, in the end, on each of us.

NOTES

I am grateful to my colleagues in the Natural Assets Project, and in particular to Barry Shelley, for helping to stimulate many of the ideas discussed in this chapter.

1. This is not to say that the degree of intra-generational equity has no impact on environmental quality for future generations. As discussed in Chapter 4, wide disparities of power

and wealth can accelerate environmental degradation by raising the rate of time prefer-ence applied to natural resources by both the poor and the rich. For a discussion of the implications of the rights of future generations for our conception of property rights to land and natural resources, see McGregor (1999).

2. The quotation is from the constitution of the state of Montana in the United States. For examples of similar statements from national constitutions around the world, see Chapter 2.

3. Both identifications characteristically invoke idealized pictures of the market and the state. 'Proponents of central planning tend to compare the market as it actually works with the government as it would work under ideal circumstances,' observes an ardent champion of the market (De Alessi 1998: 3). Yet in the same fashion, proponents of the market tend to compare the state (or 'central planning,' as they prefer to label it) as it actually works with the market as it would work under ideal circumstances. The same author claims, for example, that 'the existence of a market in which private rights can be exchanged implies that future consequences are instantaneously capitalized into current transfer prices and reflected in owners' wealth' (ibid.: 10).

4. Injustice has also figured among these aims; for example, in the hundred years between the Civil War and the Civil Rights Act, property rights often incorporated restrictions aimed to enforce racial segregation and discrimination. For a historical account of the tensions between sanctified and instrumental conceptions of property rights, see Friedman (2001).

5. Indeed, some have attempted to define the withdrawal of such givings as a 'taking.' For example, the *Wall Street Journal* (McCoy 1995) reports that corporate farmers in Califor-nia's Central Valley who get subsidized water to irrigate their crops have demanded compensation for federal and state regulations that would divert some of this water to restore salmon runs. 'We have a right to that water,' a top farm lobbyist insists, 'and if the government wants it for fish, they have to pay us.' The *Journal* reports that 'the corporate farmers could claim reimbursement at market rates – meaning reimbursement out of the federal treasury at rates 10 times the subsidized rate they now pay.'

6. See, for example, Sherraden (1991) and Oliver and Shapiro (1995).

7. See Mittal (2000). This reflects more general biases in US farm support programs; see Williams-Derry (2000).

8. For a discussion of the bundle-of-sticks metaphor in property law, see Ross (1989).

9. Barnes and Breslow (2001) calculate that the majority of households would receive more in dividends than they would pay in higher fuel prices. With the fees calibrated to cut carbon emissions to meet the targets in the Kyoto global climate accord, the net effect of the sky trust would be to increase the net incomes of the poorest 10 percent of families in the USA by about 5 percent, while reducing those of the richest 10 percent by 1 percent.

10. For discussion, see Best (2001) and Danks (2001).

REFERENCES

Agarwal, Anil and Narain, Sunita (2000), 'Redressing ecological poverty through participatory democracy: Case studies from India,' Working Paper DPE-00-01, Amherst, MA: Political Economy Research Institute, December.

Baer, Paul; Harte, John; Haya, Barbara; Herzog, Antonia V.; Holdren, John; Hultman, Nathan E.; Kammen, Daniel M.; Norgaard, Richard B.; and Raymond, Leigh (2000), 'Equity and greenhouse gas responsibility,' *Science*, 289 (29 September): 2287.

Barnes, Peter and Breslow, Marc (2001), 'Pie in the sky? The battle for atmospheric scarcity rent,' Working Paper DPE-01-05, Amherst, MA: Political Economy Re-search Institute, February.

Best, Constance (2001), 'Values, markets, and rights: rebuilding forest ecosystem assets,' in James K. Boyce and Barry Shelley (eds), *Natural Assets: Democratizing Environmental Ownership*, forthcoming.

Bromley, Daniel (1993), 'Regulatory takings: Coherent concept or logical contradiction', *Vermont Law Review*, 17(3): 647–82.

Danks, Cecilia (2001) 'Community-based stewardship: A way to invest in forests and forest communities,' in James K. Boyce and Barry Shelley (eds), *Natural Assets: Democratizing Environmental Ownership*, forthcoming.

De Alessi, Louis (1998), 'Private property rights as the basis for free market environmentalism,' in Peter J. Hill and Roger E. Meiners (eds), *Who Owns the Environment?*, Lanham, MD: Rowman & Littlefield, pp. 1–36.

Dixon, K.A. (2001), 'Reclaiming brownfields: From corporate liability to community asset,' Working Paper DPE-01-01, Amherst, MA: Political Economy Research Institute, January.

Friedman, Gerald (2001), 'The sanctity of property in American economic history,' Working Paper DPE-01-04, Amherst, MA: Political Economy Research Institute, February.

Goodstein, Eban S. (1999), *Economics and the Environment*, 2nd edn, New York: Simon & Schuster.

Jansson, AnnMari, Hammer, Monica, Folke, Carl and Costanza, Robert (eds) (1994), *Investing in Natural Capital: The Ecological Economics Approach to Sustainability*, Washington, DC: Island Press.

King, Martin Luther, Jr (1965), 'Remaining Awake Through a Great Revolution,' commencement address for Oberlin College, Oberlin, Ohio, June.

McCoy, Charles (1995) 'Private matter: The push to expand property rights stirs both hopes and fears,' *Wall Street Journal*, 4 April: A1, A14.

McGregor, Joan L. (1999), 'Property rights and environmental protection: Is this land made for you and me?', *Arizona State Law Journal*, 31(2): 391–437.

Medoff, Peter and Sklar, Holly (1994), *Streets of Hope: The Fall and Rise of an Urban Neighborhood*, Boston, MA: South End Press.

Mittal, Aunradha (2000), 'The last plantation,' Oakland: Institute for Food and Development Policy, Backgrounder 6(1).

Oliver, Melvin L. and Shapiro, Thomas M. (1995), *Black Wealth/White Wealth: A New Perspective on Racial Inequality*, New York: Routledge.

Ross, Thomas (1989), 'Metaphor and paradox,' *Georgia Law Review*, 23: 1053–84.

Sherraden, Michael (1991), *Assets and the Poor: A New American Welfare Policy*, New York: M.E. Sharpe.

Williams-Derry, Clark (2000), *Green Acres: How Taxpayers are Subsidizing the Demise of the Family Farm*, Washington, DC: Environmental Working Group.

Name index

Subject index

ability to pay 15, 18, 39
acequias 4
agenda power 8
agriculture *see* crops, domestication of;
    jute; maize; rice; sustainable
    agriculture
air pollution 3, 9, 39–41, 53, 55–6,
    58–61, 67, 90, 92–3, 127, 134
appropriation 8, 114–5, 131, 133–4
atrazine 95, 100
automobile industry 41

Bangladesh 29, 30, 37, 89–90, 93
benefit-cost analysis *see* cost-benefit
    analysis
biodiversity *see* biological diversity
biological diversity 42, 90, 97, 104, 106,
    109–11, 117
    see also crop genetic diversity
birth control 29
Brazil 26–7, 90, 120
brownfields 133

campesinos 94, 96, 98–9, 133
carbon dioxide emissions 30, 90–2, 109,
    133–4
cattle ranching 26–7, 39, 107
Churchill, Winston 128
class 36, 51–2, 67, 81
civil liberties 52, 55, 59, 62
Coasian bargaining 35–6, 85
collective action 36, 84–5, 118
command and control 127
common property 7–8
Commission for Racial Justice 45
comparative advantage 88, 99
compensation test 24, 34
composition effect 47, 49, 61, 64–5
consumer sovereignty 8
consumption 6, 25

consumers' surplus 34, 38, 50–1, 67,
    70–1
corn *see* maize
cost-benefit analysis 17, 19, 34, 36,
    38–9, 50, 70, 108
Costa Rica 27, 30, 54
crop genetic diversity 22, 88–9, 93,
    96–8, 100, 131, 133
crops, domestication of 3, 93

decision power 8
deep ecology 2
deforestation 38, 110, 118
    in the Amazon 26
    in Central America 26
    in the Philippines 43–4, 104–9,
        111–8
    in southeast Asia 26
demand for environmental quality 6, 45,
    50–1, 71, 61–2
democracy 43–4, 83, 118, 125–8
democratization 11, 83, 125–6, 131
demographic transition 29
disaster vulnerability 14–5, 17–9
discount rate *see* time horizons
distribution
    of income 5, 6, 38
    of power 1, 22–3, 36, 38, 43, 55,
        60–2, 65, 67–9, 71–4, 79–83,
        111, 114, 117–8, 128, 130
    of wealth 1, 17, 23, 111, 117, 128
    see also redistribution
diversity 98
    see also biological diversity
Dudley Street Neighborhood Initiative
    132

ecological economics 22
ecological poverty 132
ecological restoration 3, 132